How to Draw a Map of the Forest:

Volume VI of
The Travels of
Senator & Wendy V

- © 2015 by Wendy V. All rights reserved. No part of this publication may be reproduced or transmitted in any form or by any means, electronic or mechanical, including photocopy, recording, or any information storage and retrieval system, without the prior written consent of the author and/or publisher.

- Cover photography © 2013 by David Zuchowski. Cover design © 2015 by Wendy V.

ISBN: 978-0-99150-936-2

Other Titles by Wendy V

Travelogues:
How to Read a Compass in the Dark (2006)

How to Change a Flat on a Unicycle (2007)

How to Start a Fire Under the Sea (2009)

How to Eat a Pizza From a Can (2011)

How to Hitch a Ride With No Thumbs (2013)

Poetry:
Eventually, Finally (2007)

for Senator—

...because I knew you long before I met you...

"I haven't been everywhere, but it's on my list."

~Susan Sontag

Table of Contents

Introduction	i
Dewey or Not?	1
Trapped in Paradise and Other Inconveniences	29
Just Bluffin'	103
Climb Every Mountain, or At Least Attempt One	127
Afterword	181
Appendix A: Dick Giracco Memoir	183
Appendix B: Kailua Update	187

Author's Note

This book can be understood and even enjoyed without having perused the previous five in the series, but why in the world would you want to deprive yourself in such a way?

Introduction

It's a funny thing when you tell people that you have been to all fifty states. You tend to receive one of three possible reactions. Most people offer a sincere and pleasantly surprised congratulatory response, garnished with wistful imagination if they happen to enjoy traveling themselves. Others seem quizzical and somewhat apprehensive, as though you have told them that you finally mastered the art of découpage. They can't comprehend why someone would choose to do such a thing, and frankly, they are a little suspicious of anyone who has. Finally, there are those lost in the statement itself, but that's another book altogether. ("You say there are *fifty* states?...")

After two years together, Senator and I had been to almost half of the United States. It took another eight years to conquer the rest. When our plane landed in Hawaii in July of 2013, I experienced an immense sense of accomplishment. Yes, I realized that I had not done anything especially grand by stepping onto state number fifty. In fact, my part in the project had basically entailed sitting on my rear for the previous nine hours, flying through the air in a metal tube. None of my travels had brought me wealth (quite the opposite), given me a recognizable name, or done much for the human race. Hence, it was understandable that the captain, co-pilot, flight attendants, and hundreds of other passengers were unimpressed, noting my presence only with an automatic nod as I exited the aircraft.

Still, it was an accomplishment in that, in an instant, I had realized a lifelong aspiration. Though I had not focused on it as a daily obsession, it was something that had been part of me as long as I could remember. Coming from a girl who was thrilled to receive her very own globe at five years old, that is a long time. In many ways, it meant more to me than graduating from college. (Four of my professors just fainted.) In this education, I, along with my Essential Other, had been the professors. The country was our classroom, the land, people, food, and culture our curriculum. All of the textbooks were three-dimensional, and critical thinking and problem-solving skills were constantly at the forefront. I challenge anyone to find a better school. Best of all, 'graduation' left me yearning for more. Thus, book number six...

~Wendy V
September 2013

Chapter 1
Dewey or Not?:
Early July 2013

Somehow in the midst of day-to-day events large and small, another calendar page had been exhausted. Stealthily, the last few days of May had slipped away, revealing June 1st. I half-smiled at the bold, blocky number "10" that I had drawn on the noteworthy Saturday. It was our anniversary. Senator and I had spent the previous decade first befriending each other, then rescuing each other, and then building a life together.

On one hand, it had flown by. On the other hand, it seemed hardly possible that we had crammed so much into *just* ten years. On the third hand (which it would have been handy to have, given the mad pace that was now second nature), so much was still new. Senator's live recordings were live indeed, taking on something of a life of their own. More dates were scheduled, more music documented, and more sleep lost. I would be lying if I said that it was always easy, or that every show always went according to plan, but wouldn't it be stale if we never faced a challenge?

In late June, the annual Okka jazz festival rolled around once again in Milwaukee, and for the fourth year in a row we recorded it. All of it, that is, including two additional sets that were added for the first time. As in years past, there was a certain homecoming atmosphere, bonding musicians, the supportive audience, and those of us fortunate enough to be working at the festival.* We had a wonderful time and it was a successful venture from the technological standpoint, but by Sunday night we had to pack up the gear and head home. Work came early the next day, but at least only a few days remained until our first summer off together, sans any retail job.

Depending on the way the months and school year fall, I either have five or six weeks off every summer. I do not take the time for granted, nor do I waste it. Now, an entirely new dimension had been added. My best friend and roommate would be around... all the time. The prospect thrilled me, because it seemed for the first time since we had met, we might actually have enough time together. A small part of me hoped that I was not being naive, though. Would too much of a good thing backfire?

As it turned out, I need not have held any concern. The summer flew by even faster than usual. We had quickly adapted to our temporary routine of sleeping in, working around the house, and then recording or watching

---

* Special thanks to Adrienne Pierluissi and Bruno Johnson of Okka Disk and The Sugar Maple in Milwaukee for bringing world-class experimental music together in such a warm setting. At one point on that Saturday night in June, their efforts saw the realization of drummers from three different continents improvising together.

black-and-white movies. Truth be told, I missed him like crazy when I had to go back to work. Before that time crept up however, we squeezed in a few more travels.

*   *   *

We had been to Door County, Wisconsin, to visit our friends before, but with the new liberty of not having to sandwich free time in between retail hours, we decided to take four nights, extending time with friends and the inviting landscape of coastline, trees, and meadows. On a Sunday morning we loaded up our gear and secured our bikes to the back of Senator's car. It puts an entirely different and welcome spin on a vacation when you are not exhausted from working late the night before, and you know that you don't have to be back at work the morning after arriving home. I glanced at Senator; he looked carefree, lightly tanned from numerous bike rides, and ready to go play on the peninsula.

As is our routine, we brought a bag of fruit to nibble on the ride. About an hour into the drive, Senator asked me to pass him an apple. I reached in and selected a gala. As is also our routine, once he finishes his fruit, he donates the remains (cores, stems, peels, etc.) to the earth, since they are biodegradable. If he is the one driving, this generally entails me rolling down my passenger side window, sitting back, and waiting for the appropriate moment. At an instant that he determines, the inedible parts of the produce are launched.*

---

* I have had some difficulty mastering this skill. My first attempt involved tossing pistachio shells out of my window, only to find them scattered in my back seat the next time I stopped. Clearly I

And so it was that he finished his apple and nodded for me to roll down the necessary window. I did so. He briefly surveyed the situation one more time, and then let the fruit fly. I'm not quite sure what went wrong in that moment, but the apple core was instantly separated into four or five pieces, which landed in various locations within my realm of the car. That wasn't supposed to happen. A small chunk skidded across my face, while another smacked into the dashboard. I brushed more apple mush off of the map I had been consulting, noting that the main piece, at least, seemed to have made a successful journey to the roadside. "Oops..." observed Senator. Inconvenient and messy, yet hysterically funny, I could only laugh.

    I grabbed a wet wipe and cleaned my face. It occurred to me, with some chagrin, that these are the moments, if accidentally captured on video, that make people famous. Forget the accomplishments and great feats of humanity. It is the twenty-first century; your fifteen seconds of fame can be immortalized on YouTube. Sometimes this is due to nothing more than a misjudged apple core.

    The rest of the six-hour trip went quickly, and we were soon among the familiar county roads. I called our friend Marge and told her that we were about half an hour away. As we drove up the Lake Michigan side, the temperature and humidity continued to drop to a very

---

had forgotten to account for wind resistance. (I understand even great scientists make this mistake when engaged in the throes of a delightfully salty snack.)

comfortable level. We turned off the air conditioning and rolled our windows down. "Remind me again why we live in ILLinois?"

The old white farmhouse where Bill and Marge have stayed each summer for the past many years looked the same. The owner was not known for maintaining current trends in decorating, but the home had its own charm nonetheless. Our friends greeted us excitedly, and we went into our four-people-talking-at-once brand of planning, catching up, and goofing around.*

When the welcomes died down, I went upstairs to make up our bed. Senator unpacked some goodies we had brought to share. At home, dessert happens maybe twice a month. On vacation with friends, a daily confection was deemed necessary. Similarly and obviously, ample cheese must always be included.

After unpacking, it was still early enough for an inaugural bike ride. We filled our water bottles and

---

* Coming from a family where interrupting is a viable form of communication, I don't necessarily consider it rude behavior. Still, to be fair and effective, it must conform to distinct guidelines. The Interrupter's volume must never exceed that of the Interruptee. (This rule however, if broken, is easily remedied by the Interruptee adjusting his/her volume accordingly. Eventually a happy balance will ensue.) Likewise, the Interrupter may interject at any point, so long as his/her message is at least as urgent as that of the Interruptee. (This rule can be a bit tricky to navigate if there are no neutral third parties who might determine the hierarchy of verbal importance. In fact, this rule can be extremely tricky to navigate if said third party is concurrently acting as a Secondary Interrupter.) Although I won't get into advanced technique at this time, you may contact me for details if you share my Italian or Slovak heritage.

hopped on, turning out of the driveway to the main road. Just a half block later, the main road turned away from us, leaving us on a quieter stretch. We pedaled along fields and past a few houses. Though we had been this way before, I was struck by a new sight.

Out grazing in the fields we saw some brown animals that almost looked like small deer. They did not move like deer, though. We decided to investigate. Once we had stopped, it became clear that the animals in question were actually some sort of very large bird. They looked as though they had wandered through a portal out of prehistoric times. We have large herons at home, but they are thin, graceful, and tend to be loners. These creatures-- whose name I never did find out-- were bigger, sturdier, and clustered in gangs. They were not aggressive at all, but I'm fairly sure I could have ridden one around if I could have lassoed it.

We climbed back on our bikes and finished our ride. It was time to get back to the house anyway. We had to get ready for the evening's events, which included a casual barn concert. First on the agenda was a bite to eat, though, so we joined Bill and Marge, setting off for Stillwell's.

Stillwell's can best be described as a burger joint that wandered out of the Midwest, lost its way, and one day found itself in southern Florida. There it stayed. Except it's in northern Wisconsin. The tropical-themed patio held several outdoor tables, all of which were very high off of the ground for some reason.* Ordering took place at a

---

* Perhaps it was so one could enjoy the tropics even when there was a foot of snow on the ground.

walk-up counter, so we looked over the menu and made our selections. Surprisingly, there were homemade veggie burgers in the tropics.

As we waited for our number to be called, we staked our claim at one of the tables. I awkwardly jumped up and swung my leg over the bench, in what must have looked like a city slicker's attempt at mounting a horse. I could almost hear the cowboy music playing as the narrator crooned his voice over: "The sun was beginning its long descent in the Door County tropics, as the posse patiently awaited their grub..." I glanced around the patio as the men folk readied the recorder.

Podcasting had become a mild obsession the last time we were in Door County with Bill and Marge, yielding ten episodes of impromptu, unedited, and generally funny conversation for the ears of anyone who enjoys the relaxed and random. We were now on track to repeat this pattern during the next four days. Senator set up the small machine and adjusted the microphones. Bill noted the time, keeping us in line with the thirty minute (give or take) time limit.

Beside the requisite tiki torches and two-dimensional parrots, there were signs everywhere, all pleading the same thing. "PLEASE do not throw out baskets!!!" Three exclamation points were serious indeed. Apparently there had been a rash of customers with diabolical practices. Were they too stupid to realize that the commonly seen red plastic baskets were actually serviceware, and not garbage? Were their plans more sinister, involving a plot to max out landfills and ruin the ecology, one burger basket at a time?

Or perhaps the baskets were not being thrown out, but unapologetically stolen. Whatever the case, the situation was desperate. Obviously there had not even been enough time to type the signs, which were scrawled in marker.

I pictured the staff meeting that I could only assume had led to this. Everyone was dressed in Hawaiian shirts. The boss wore a straw hat and had a cardboard parrot on his shoulder. *Margaritaville* played in the background, drowning out the neighbor's radio, which was broadcasting a countdown to the first Packers game of the season. "Ladies and Gentlemen, we have a grave situation before us..." began the manager. *...Wastin' away again...* "I never thought I'd see this day, but we are down to our last four baskets. Yes, I know. You've all worked hard, and many of you have repeatedly asked customers to kindly leave their used baskets atop the garbage can. Joe, I remember the day you built that nice tray on top of it to hold the baskets. But it just hasn't been enough." *...Some people claim that there's...* "And so, at this time, I am going to ask each of you to take the paper and the marker that I've placed before you, and make a sign. Not just any sign; this needs to be a sign that people will notice! Be bold. Send a message! We cannot sacrifice any more baskets. People, we are on the verge of ruin, and it's up to all of us to end this madness!" *...It's my own damn fault...* Thus, the signs were born, posted at various strategic points around the patio, and most noticeably on Joe's basket tray.

Soon our numbers were called and our hearty burgers picked up. In between mouthfuls, we recorded a half hour of who knows what. On the west side of the patio the sun was setting, outlining the ersatz palm trees. We wrapped up the last moments of our podcast, and believe me, not one of our baskets was thrown away. We were all going to bed with a clear conscience that night.

After dinner it was time for the barn concert. Located on the other end of the same property on which we were staying was a restored two-story wooden barn. Throughout the summer, the owner hosted concerts of various genres, including folk, bluegrass, reggae, pop, etc. On this particular night, the featured artist was Karen Mal, a singer/songwriter who played guitar and mandolin.

Karen turned out to be a true talent, whose songs ranged from tender, to quirky, to just plain folksy. Though it wasn't my first choice in style, I, along with the others, enjoyed her concert very much. I especially liked the work of one of her guests, named David Stoddard. David's melodies, thought-provoking content, and interplay with Karen just about converted me to a full-fledged folk enthusiast.

Not everyone was so appreciative. Despite an audience that was composed of 95% respectful patrons, we had the misfortune to sit in the same row as the loudmouths. Though the atmosphere was casual, I could have done without the obnoxious, incessant chatting and joking by two couples a few seats away. I glared at them-- hard. So did others. Even the easygoing, lighthearted postmodern hippies on stage were getting slightly annoyed. It was getting out-of-hand. Conscious that a broad four-person slap-down (a la Three Stooges) might embarrass my companions, I opted for concentrating my mental powers on making the jerks leave. I narrowed my eyes and furrowed my brow. I'm not sure I can take credit, but after another song they left, thankfully. The hippies breathed a sigh of relief, content at not having witnessed violence in the name of preserving folk tradition.

The concert ended and we walked back to the farmhouse. We were feeling pretty good, in part because of the great music* and in part because sweets and a serial awaited us. We discussed the many options for both. Unanimously we decided to make Bill choose. Thus, carrot cake and the first two episodes of *Jungle Jim*† it was.

Some time later we awoke from the deep sleep that had ensconced us somewhere around the 7-minute mark of the dvd. We stretched our limbs and popped things back into their rightful places, as opposed to how the outline of the couch had left them. Our friends were tired too, so we all said our good-nights and parted company. Senator and I climbed the steep stairs to our bedroom, noting the light rain that had begun outside the window at the top of the stairs.

"Should we close our window?" I asked, a little disappointed at the prospect.

"Well, nothing's coming in. I say leave 'em open." *Good call, Senator.* We crawled into bed as a cool breeze flew across the screens. Later the lightning started. Still later loud claps of thunder woke us up. The rain pounded down

---

* The final number included a tiny special guest, Karen's baby. Upon being woken up from a nap, the infant joined her by blowing into a harmonica on cue.

† including various stuffed tigers and a heroine who looked like she should be on a beach in Malibu

throughout the night, but never came in. Pure slumbering heaven.

*   *   *

Marge and I are often pleased to learn how alike we think. It is not that we are vain, or that we think our way is best,* but we have a certain affinity for planning and execution that has brought to fruition some very fun excursions for us and our Essential Others. Because we are strategists, we are also realists. That does not mean we are pessimists, but simply that we plan for everything.† Hence, it is our pattern to plan the most involved adventure on the first full day we have together in Door County, allowing us a few back-up days in case of bad weather, illness, ferry collisions, etc..

We agreed that Monday should be Rock Island State Park adventure day. As we sipped our coffee and watched the rain trickle down the picture window however, we were thrown for a small loop. We could postpone the plans, but the showers seemed to be moving off, which would leave perfect hiking weather. Plus, the weather was iffy for the next two days, according to the only-occasionally-accurate-yet-somehow-always-revered Weather Channel. On the other hand, we might dampen the mood (not to mention our sammiches‡) if we dragged Bill and Senator through the

---

* Although, well, to be honest...

† Should you need any odd assortment of items ranging from bandaids to batteries, to ferry schedules, to sunscreen, to cheese, they are sure to be found in either my backpack or hers.

‡ Based on everything we have learned from World War II-era serial films, nobody but nobody says "sandwiches". We prefer to keep the traditional "sammich" alive and well.

mist only to hike in a downpour once we were on the isolated island. We could definitely lose some points there, just when we thought we had covered all angles. (Strategists, you see, are not often gamblers by nature, despite scads of military leader-types in the movies.)

Faced with a decision that would affect everyone, we sought the boys' input. "So, what do you guys think?" ventured Marge, proceeding to point out the pros and cons of going on either Monday or Tuesday.

Before she could spell out her second invisible bullet point, Senator chimed in with a hearty, "I dunno know; whatever you think..."

Bill offered an equally staunch opinion. "Whatever you think, Honey. I'm not sure..."

Well, we tried. I looked at Marge and I could tell she was up for a challenge, so I bit. "I say we go. There's no lightning, so the worst that can happen is we get wet." For good measure I threw in "Plus, the gray skies might scare away a few of the tourists. We might have the place to ourselves." And for my grand finale: "Remember how neat it was crossing the water in the fog?" Thinking back to our satisfyingly ferryboat ride a few years back, Marge had made up her mind to go, too.

Five minutes after we were in the car, the sun came out. Contrary to the weather at home, we found that once the sun came out, the humidity instantly disappeared. This pattern repeated several times during the trip. Where we live, sunny interludes between rain spells mean multiplied humidity and general yuckiness. Apparently others understood this weather anomaly, because the tourists were not scared away. At any rate, we were off for a beautiful day on the island.

As in the past, we drove north up the county to the Washington Island ferry port. This time however, we opted to take a car over, instead of our bikes. It would save us about twelve miles of pedaling, as well as give us more time to explore the state park. The gathering clouds may have also influenced the decision.

Bill drove the car up the ramp and onto the boat. One by one we squeezed our way out of the doors, which were practically touching the car and wall on either side of us. We had to catch our balance because the boat had started rocking and swaying... and swaying and rocking... We pitched back and forth, making an interesting backdrop for a short video Bill took. In it you can see the remaining three of us standing in front of the railing. Like clockwork, the lake rises blackish-gray behind us, disappears, and then returns on cue. Good thing no one was prone to sea sickness.

When he finished filming, Bill joined us to look over the water. Scattered around were floating little silvery-white fish. By "floating" I mean they were dead, as opposed to reclining comfortably while riding the waves. The more we looked, the more we saw. After much discussion and some drizzle, our group developed the theory that the fish-no-more could be the result of lightning striking the water during the previous night's storm. I was a little skeptical, but I had to admit that I had nothing better. Just as I had given up trying to understand why some fish would be effected while others continued to swim around merrily, we arrived on Washington Island. Once again we sucked in our guts and gingerly slid into the car. After disembarking, Bill drove us to the opposite end of the island, where we could catch the ferry to Rock Island. As long as we had the convenience of a car, we made a pit stop at the local grocery store for some lunch items on the way. Though I don't remember the name of the place, it carried all of the regular staples, as well as an extensive assortment of Scandinavian essentials. We made our selections and drove on to the ferry dock parking lot.

As we waited for the boat, it began to rain lightly. It was too late to do anything about it now; we were about to go strand ourselves in a remote location where even bicycles weren't allowed. As it turned out, we weren't the only ones up for some adventure. A woman with some cumbersome gear asked if we had ever been to Rock Island before, specifically to the lighthouse. Why, yes, indeed we had-- just last summer. She then asked about the walk to the lighthouse, since she would be staying there a week as the keeper. Bill piped up to give her the real scoop. "Oh, you mean the Trail of Tears? It was a lot more involved than we were told, as we found out. You've got quite a trek ahead of you. But you might be able to ask the ranger over there to give you a ride in his golf cart." It all sounded accurate until he added, "...His name's Jimmy."

The cheerful woman thanked us and wandered toward the approaching ferry. I jerked my head toward Bill after she had left. "You don't know his name! You just made that up last year!" Indeed Bill had dubbed the ranger "Lyin' Jimmy"-- not to his face-- after the ranger had told us it was just a short walk to the lighthouse, and after he had proceeded to drive past us in his comfortable golf cart.

"Yeah, but she don't know that," Bill reasoned casually. He had me there.

The rain continued to fall during our 15-minute voyage o'er the choppy sea. Soon we landed on Rock Island, where the rain picked up steadily. Fortunately, we claimed via squatter's rights the only picnic shelter within sight. By the time we settled ourselves under it, it was pouring.

When the skies have opened up generously, and your little band is hungry and silly and wet beyond caring, two activities take precedence: eating and podcasting. I voiced my objections that the listeners might not appreciate an episode dedicated to us talking and laughing with food in our mouths, but I was soundly outvoted.* Daver set up the recording device while I unpacked the centerpiece of the feast-- the knackbröd.

All of the usual suspects (cheese, olives, cheese, horseradish, veggie spread, cheese, antipasto) comprised the picnic, but the knackbröd was king, simply because it was the strangest. In my hands I held a paper-wrapped disc about a foot in diameter and about an inch and a half thick. It would have made a nice frisbee on a sunnier day. The contents were plain: rye flour, water, salt. We took turns guessing its format. Marge believed that it was quartered into four pieces. Bill or Senator suggested that it was many more pieces, just packaged together. I was

---

* To be fair, the episode turned out much better than I could have imagined. It was even funny, if garbled at times.

holding out for one giant rye cracker. Finally we broke open the seal, with no less anticipation than children attacking their first Christmas present of the year.

Simultaneously we burst into laughter, yielding a few quizzical looks from the people who had commandeered the only other table under the shelter.* Marge won for accuracy, as the knackbröd was indeed divided into four sections. I was somewhat on the right trail however, in picturing the ridiculousness of a giant cracker. The knackbröd was not cut into wedges, but sliced into four giant discs. Without prompting, everyone reached for his or her rye circle, (which now resembled a thick, flat, brown paper plate,) and the collective maturity level dropped to about eight years old. Oh, and I forgot to mention that each one had a small hole in the center, about an inch in diameter. This multiplied the entertainment value significantly, not unlike a mega butter cookie.

Eventually we had feasted on enough knackbröd and other accessories to satisfy even the hungriest Swede-Italian. The rain was finally letting up, so we started down a path through the meadow. Before we reached the campground at the end of it, we turned into the sparse woods, which led to the shoreline. In the woods we found an old cemetery with just a few graves. The stones were barely legible and belonged to people who had passed away in the mid-nineteenth century. Prior to that, the land was a Native American burial ground.

No ghosts haunted us, but we would have preferred them over the pests we were about to encounter.

---

* poor them

Continuing on the overgrown path, we soon reached the sandy beach. The sun was shining brightly by this point, and the water was sparkling. We meandered around through the sea grasses, finally perching ourselves on a driftwood log. We began another podcasting episode, until one by one we were attacked by biting black flies.* They started out as an annoyance but quickly progressed to a merciless invasion. This ushered in the birth of the *On the Move* podcast, as we hurried our way back through the woods away from the beach. We had one more stop to explore before leaving the island, anyway.

The only notable structure left on the island from its days as a private haven was a large stone boathouse. The main level opened to an immense Viking-style dining hall, complete with chunky, beautifully hand-carved wooden furniture, a horned chandelier, and a fireplace worthy of Charles Foster Kane. Around the outskirts of the room and in a balcony overhead, there were a few displays depicting the owner's Icelandic heritage. The lower level sat on the water, once providing a sort of float-in garage for rich playmates to park their boats.

It was while I was examining the artifacts and historical displays that I met Dewey. Marge was playing an old piano in the corner of the room. Senator was busy wandering around with his camera, and Bill was relaxing on a nearby bench. So no one noticed at first when the dark-haired, intensely blue-eyed boy of about five started following me around.

---

* Why is it necessary to specify *black* flies? Are there really flies of any other color? I'd like to see a yellow one.

He was very interested in all of the artifacts, and asked me lots of questions in between sliding a dead cricket around like a race car along the edges of the display cases. Going into full teacher mode, I answered every question as well as I could. The more I talked, the more interested he became. I was amazed at his attention span, but I started to wonder where the kid's parents were. We had seen no other adults who might have belonged to him, and it was a long way back to the campground. It was also a dangerously short distance to the water.

He continued our conversation, morphing the cricket into an unwitting action figure, who was apparently interested in history. Finally he stopped and stared at me, and then asked grandly, "How do you know so much *stuff*?" I beamed. I was vindicated. A few years of college and a lifetime of curiosity and fascination with trivial facts had not gone unnoticed. Where were my high school students to hear this?

Our final stop was in a very small room that held some books, a few articles of clothing, and a typewriter. Dewey was completely taken by the typewriter, whose carriage his generation would never have to remember to return. He also wanted to know about the book, so I explained that it was written in Icelandic and translated into English, not sure if he understood that there were different languages. "I spoke some Russian when I was little," he informed me very matter-of-factly.

"Oh?..." was all I could say.

"Yes, I'm Russian and I'm two things but I can't remember the other one," he continued. I was trying to wrap my brain around this response, and possibly formulate an adoption plan if his parents did not show up soon. Just then he added wistfully, "I wish I was Polish..."

And there you have it. I never did find any adult who claimed him. In fact, I never even knew his name. When I told Senator and our friends about him, they decided he must be Dewey, or Dewey's ghost more accurately. Dewey had been a relative (son perhaps?) of Mr. Thordardson, the prosperous owner of Rock Island in days long gone. I guess that would explain having a dead cricket for a pet...

We took our last glance around Rock Island. It was easy to see all of its natural beauty in the now brightly shining sun. Along with a few others, we climbed onto the small ferry back to Washington Island. There we found Bill's car waiting to convey us to the other side. Of course, there just might be one stop for milk shakes, or in our case, a shared coffee malted.

As in years past, the ferry ride to the mainland was a relaxing half hour. Being that I remember nothing about it, it is also very possible that I was asleep for most of it. That, combined with a leisurely drive back to the house was enough to recharge our batteries. Senator and I broke ranks for a quick bike ride to take advantage of our second wind.

We actually had ulterior motives. The last time we had gone east down the road, we had noticed a farmhouse that sold pure maple syrup. Always enticed by this delicacy, we wanted to stop and at least check out the prices. It turned out to be a good investment as the owner charged far less than we generally paid in the store. As the kind senior citizen led us to her sugar shack, she informed us that it was the last of the spring's batch. She explained that once the buds are on the maple trees, it's too late for good syrup. Since it was July, she only had about fifteen or twenty bottles left. We bought half a gallon's worth. Now that I have tasted it, we should have bought it all, although it was challenging enough to transport the half gallon on a bike.

Following the brief syrup run, Senator and Marge practiced musical arrangements, on guitar and keyboard respectively. They were toying with the idea of forming a duo to play some nicer casual establishments near our hometowns. Bill and I chatted and knocked out another episode of *On the Lam*, inadvertently capturing their informal rehearsal. When the hour expired, so did the knackbröd; we were all hungry.

A few miles away was a comfortable restaurant that served upper-end pub fare. We snagged the last available outside table, from which we could see Lake Michigan just across the main street of the small town. We ordered our meal, and sat back to visit and plan the next day. The food was tasty, but what I will never forget is watching the fog roll in.

Prior to that evening, I had used the expression loosely to refer to any fog that had settled over the land. Never again. When ship captains use the verb 'roll', they mean a mighty, foreboding wall of mist that moves from the water onto the land in a swift, calculating move, obscuring all in its path. If we were not so intrigued by the site, it might have been unsettling to go from a clear sunset to such reduced visibility in a matter of thirty minutes. It was going to be a great night for falling asleep on the couch to another movie...

*   *   *

I was up and down throughout the night, mostly wondering why I was up and down. I soon remembered that it always takes a good twenty-four hours or so before my stomach rebels against too many rich indulgences. It doesn't make me sick, but it lets me know it is not pleased. *You don't treat me like this at home*, it whines. *Shut up; we're on vacation!* I respond unsympathetically.

Being born and raised American, I had shrugged it all off by morning. My blissful amnesia allowed me to sit with Marge at the kitchen table and make our plans for the day ahead... which would surely include more good food. Spoiled by the rugged beauty of Rock Island, we suggested a trip to Newport State Park. It would be Senator's and my first time there, but based on the online reviews, we would love it. Everyone in cyberspace agreed that it was scenic, clean, easy to get to, and good for hiking and picnicking. The only complaint was that it was "too remote" and that you "hardly ever saw anyone there". That was perhaps the most enticing of all of its qualities.

As you should know by now, a proper Door County picnic requires pit stops at the Door County Bakery (for Corsica Bread) and Koepsel's (for everything else).* Once again we loaded up on an assortment of all things savory, hearty, pickled, and sweet. Among the treasures, of course, were two varieties of pickled garlic to suit Marge and

---

* If it's delicious and comes in a glass jar, you will find it at Koepsel's.

Senator. The four of us carried our armloads to the car, eager to get started.

When we arrived at the park, it took a few minutes to get situated and scout out the best spot. As Senator gathered our things, I wandered to the other side of the small parking lot to get a better look at a bike rack on someone's vehicle. I was always on the lookout for one that would work with my hatchback-style car. I got up close to see where the supports lay in relation to the window. Then I walked around each side slowly to see if it seemed secure. I did not touch anything, but I still felt pretty stupid when I realized someone had been sitting in the front seat the whole time.

Ruling out any notion I might have had of launching a career as a car thief, I joined the others for our lunch. When we had filled our bellies and repacked the leftovers, we set out for a walk. The terrain at Newport State Park is surprisingly uneven, making for a nice hike. The trail wound through the woods, up and down mildly over roots and around rocks. Most of the time Lake Michigan was in view. Though it was misting occasionally, it did not have that dreary, damp feeling to it. It was just refreshing.

When it came time for a break, we wound our way down to the beach and plopped ourselves on some rocks between sea grass and the water's edge. The visibility over the water was decreasing, but it wasn't like an overcast sky. Instead, there were several shades and layers of gray. I didn't know fog could be so colorful. Within this ideal setting, another episode of *On the Lam* was recorded.

As the drizzle ramped up and the podcasting wound

down, we stole some last moments along Lake Michigan. It was just a few steps back to the trail, but once on it, it was hard to see the water due to the increasing mist. By the time we reached the parking lot, we were very wet, but satisfied. It was far better than the dampness that we normally experience on humid July afternoons. As an added bonus, the reviewers had been correct in noting/complaining about the lack of people. We hope to return someday.

When we got 'home' and had a chance to clean up, Senator and Marge practiced some more, adding a few new tunes to their repertoire. Bill and I sat down in the tiny sun porch off the north side of the house.* He wanted to record another episode, which was fine with me, provided he first killed the too-large-for-comfort spider whose territory we had invaded. It was a productive hour† that culminated in mutual hunger. The musicians took their kitchen table curtain call, and we left to get some dinner.

Every time we go to Door County, we make it a point to stop at JJ's for dinner. It is cramped, loud, and usually involves a wait for a table, but the food is great. Patrons can choose from the Mexican or American menus. No time lost on choice there. Senator and I maintained our unbroken streak of ordering their cheese enchiladas, and as usual, we were not disappointed. Also comforting was the fact that they faithfully keep three chairs posted in the single-person bathroom.‡

---

* Yes, I am aware that this is somewhat paradoxical.
† unless you happened to be the spider
‡ See *How to Hitch a Ride With No Thumbs*

As you have surely figured out by now Reader, night life in Door County, at least with the four of us involved, is relatively calm. We tend to be in by 8:30pm or so, and no one's going to be complaining of a hangover in the morning. Still, you might be surprised at the impassioned angst that accompanies a competitive round of Yahtzee. Despite our best efforts and classiest rolls, Marge reigned supreme in this arena. We were only able to console ourselves from the heavy losses with ample cheesecake and a viewing of *The Hound of the Baskervilles*.[*]

Given that the movie was filmed in 1959, it was drenched in that rich array of color that seems more like you are watching a stage production in a theatre than a movie on a screen. Props are very ornate, yet obviously artificial. It never seems to detract from the overall visual experience, however. It is a delicate balance that I don't think could be achieved as well with modern lighting and filming methods.

At least the setting was during Doyle's intended period. For reasons I will never understand, many filmmakers choose to remove Mr. Sherlock Holmes from his Victorian era and place him in contemporary times. This dates back to at least World War II, when the revered detective's crime solving skills often conveniently aided the British in their efforts against the Nazis. Poor Sherlock has been time traveling with his pipe and violin ever since.

*   *   *

Wednesday we woke up to a dry, sunny breeze. You would think this would inspire us all to get moving, but it

---

*   starring Peter Cushing as Sherlock Holmes

was such a perfect coffee morning that we sat around for quite a while before anyone made any ambitious moves. That was fine; we were only going a few miles away to Peninsula State Park. In theory it would be the easiest of the week's excursions.

Of course, there are always the tourists. The park has a very nice paved, winding five-mile bike trail, but that does not mean it is an easy ride. For several years now we have thought of Sunset Trail as Idiot Trail. Though its creators have provided ample space for two lanes of fairly busy bicycle traffic.... Well, you can lead a horse to water, etc., etc.. People, and in particular families, cannot grasp the concept of riding single file. "Why shouldn't three people spread as wide as possible, risking a major accident with unsuspecting oncoming traffic?" they reason. "Furthermore, life should be taken at a leisurely pace. If some crazy cyclists prefer to ride at a steady clip, just about rear-ending me because I choose to stop randomly and then pedal again slowly and inconsistently, I certainly cannot be to blame," they determine. Hence, a somewhat frustrating, if always scenic, ride is afoot.

At about the two-mile mark, we rested at a lighthouse, enjoying the view of the sapphire water. After more podcasting, Senator and I rode on to the end of the trail. The beach there was very crowded, but we had only planned to stay long enough to use the bathroom anyway. We then hopped on our bikes, did a 180°, and rode back to the beginning of the Idiot Trail.

Senator had more patience than I had, or maybe he just gave up trying to find other riders who knew how to use a bike path. I rode up right behind people who blocked all lanes, loudly yelled, "On your left!", and then attempted to pass. Without fail, they were oblivious, annoying me further. I would then take any opportunity to speed past them, even if it meant straying off the path or cutting between a family. Yes, I was that fed up. Once I got going, I kept going, blowing past anyone I could. In the end, I shaved a whopping three minutes off of my ride, but at least I wasn't irritated anymore. Sweating and panting, I drank my water. Glancing up, I saw the worst of the offending families merrily coasting to the end of the line, still blocking everyone, and still smiling like idiots.

Back at the house we gave in to the only nap of our stay. After early mornings, late nights, and much activity, it was merited. Senator and Marge then practiced some more, which gave me time to read and catch up on notes. I listened as they rehearsed the songs they had been working on. It was apparent that they had a comfortable rapport as musicians as well as friends. Now they just needed a few gigs. Maybe they would even play in Door County someday.

The four of us had dinner at a small tavern on the main drag of the closest small town. Afterward we walked a few blocks to the Green Bay side of the peninsula. Meandering out along a boardwalk, we noticed a sign informing us that it was a "private dock". It was a long boardwalk, however, with no discernible possession by any one of the dozens of boats docked there, so we blatantly chose to ignore it. After all, they could always kick us out if they wanted to.*

No one troubled us for our trespassing. In fact, it was peaceful, except for the occasionally draining boats or the noisy sea gulls. We noticed that every so often a small yacht would cruise past the harbor, close to the shoreline. This begged the question of why, if one was wealthy enough to afford such luxuries, would one not sail one's boat out on the open water, versus staying so near the docks? "Perhaps they are hosting boat-watching tours?" suggested Bill. I think he may be on to something there. Much less fuss than whale- or eagle-watching. Probably more reliable, too.

By the time we drove back, the daylight had almost completely disappeared. It was the third night and dessert was a given, so we loaded up plates, grabbed the necessary silverware, and claimed our spots on the couches for *Jungle Jim*. I was already struggling to keep my eyes open. Marge was curled up in her corner, and the guys weren't far behind.

As I slipped into a dream, I barely noticed the requisite budget-conscious stuffed tigers being thrown around the on silver screen jungle. I did wake up just once during *Jungle Jim*. That brief interlude was enough to update me on the fact that the attractive blond American lead had learned that-- shock-- she was not, in fact, one of the African natives. Who knew?

*   *   *

As it had each morning with Bill and Marge, the aroma of coffee floated upstairs to our bedroom early on

---

* (better to ask forgiveness than permission)

Thursday. It was hard to believe that it was already time to pack and leave. I think it is a testament to a friendship when days spent in close proximity feel like only a few hours. Without getting too sappy, I will always treasure these times.

Senator and I went downstairs for some breakfast and last minute visiting. As we chatted, we also watched the determined squirrels enacting their grandest strategies as they attempted to hijack the bird feeder. Neither size nor logistical ability hindered their ambition. They knew what they wanted, and they went for it. Bill, Marge, Senator, and I had all been in various periods of transition during the first half of 2013. Some things were uncertain, but many possibilities awaited. Maybe there was a lesson for us somewhere among all of those aspiring and resourceful rodents.

Chapter 2
Trapped in Paradise and Other Inconveniences: Late July 2013

Hawai'i.* To decades of Americans, the very name is synonymous with paradise and escape. The idea of islands, palm trees, waterfalls, sand, surf, and beautiful people wearing grass and flowers-- which are far more exotic and stunning than mainland grass and flowers-- creates the quintessential desirable scene. Thanks in part to Hollywood, we are almost programmed to a stereotypical depiction of pleasure and ease. Go ahead. Start talking about Hawai'i to a friend or coworker and observe his/her reaction. There are sure to be wistful smiles, mild envy,

---

* I have chosen to keep the traditional spelling of Hawai'i, since in the native language the accent mark denotes the correct pronunciation. Most literature produced on the island uses this spelling as well.

and possibly a sadness at the thought of likely never getting there.

We have crowned it such a magical place that it practically does not exist. Prospective college students, when asked to name their first choice in university, will respond slyly with "University of Hawaii", neither expecting to actually go there, nor to be taken seriously by the inquisitor. Comparatively few Americans have been there, and most will never go. Still, we are fast to defend the notion of Hawai'i. And as long as we keep the lore alive, we will continue to be met with dreamy eyes and longing whenever the topic is brought up.

Senator and I, as we are fully aware, rarely have the same reactions as the masses.* The category of travel is no exception to this rule. While we wanted to see Hawai'i and looked forward to the adventure, we were not seeking the Hawai'i of the average Midwesterner's fantasy. In fact, neither of us would define paradise in terms of beaches or luaus. Instead, our purpose in planning a trip to the islands was fourfold. It was the only state which we had not visited, and how can you go to forty-nine states but not fifty? We were also curious about some natural features that only occurred there. Pearl Harbor was a destination in itself, and finally, because it was surrounded by as much myth as ocean, we wanted to see the 'real' Hawai'i. Though I was not exactly sure how to begin planning the trip, that last reason assured me that my main objective was to avoid the tourist Mecca of Waikiki.

---

* In this respect, we are very fortunate to have found each other-- two oddballs in unison.

Typically my trip planning is a standard routine of internet searches, a few phone calls to arrange lodging reservations, and an online flight booking if we are not taking our vehicle. I have a few reputable websites that I consult, and for the most part, I can guess/reason my way around from that point. Initially, I thought booking a Hawai'ian trip would run much the same. Just to be on the safe side, however, I started the process a year beforehand.

In late summer of 2011, while coming down off of the annual realization that I could not travel for at least the next nine school months, I started to think about Hawai'i. As it turns out, there is a whole lot of water between the continental U.S. and the Hawai'ian Islands. Options were simply sea or air. I thought back to our flights to the West Coast, which seemed eternal enough at four and a half hours. Then I thought of our Alaskan cruise, where we fell in love with watching the ocean float by our balcony. It was an easy decision; we would fly to southern California, and then cruise the rest of the way to Hawai'i. That would take care of most lodging, transportation, and food. Satisfied with my decision (which was approved by Senator), I shelved the planning for a few months to focus on the start my school year.

The following winter I entered phase two. This involved a casual search of cruise companies and their Hawai'ian itineraries. Here was my first snag. Because the vast majority of Americans prefer to travel to the tropics in cold months, only one company offered a cruise in July. It was not my first choice, but it was still a company I respected. Part two of the snag that was quickly stringing out the vacation sweater was that the company only ran inner-island cruises. In other words, hello nine hour flight.

I then scrolled down to crunch some numbers, which soon told me this trip would not be happening until 2013-- a year later than planned. Oh well. That would give us more time to save, and I could justify a cheaper jaunt to New Hampshire in 2012. With the new developments carefully organized and saved on the computer, I once again temporarily forgot about Hawai'i while focusing on other events in the year.

Then came that unexpected day in September 2012, when Senator learned that he would be unemployed the following January, when the store where he worked closed. Family meeting. It was unanimously agreed that we would still go to Hawai'i, but the trip would be cut to no more than a week. Despite my best efforts to make the math work, the cruise was also out. Even with accounting for accommodations, transportation, and meals, it would be cheaper to do it independently. With less than a year to plan, and many new considerations, it would truly be an adventure.

For the time being, Hawai'i was again ignored. The year progressed, and the busy holidays came and went, with the distinction of a grand send-off to Senator's retail career. When January rolled around, I reopened my vacation files, determined to have something to look forward to as the post-Christmas blahs set in. I chunked the research into four categories: flights, cars, lodging, and entertainment. None of them was as simple as it should have been.

Booking a flight required navigating its own matrix of possibilities. Was it better to connect, or to go nonstop? Which day of the week was the cheapest to fly?* What were our options for airlines? Could we save money by booking six months early, or would they give us a good deal if they were trying to fill up a plane at the last minute? What if we booked a flight, and then we couldn't find anywhere to stay?

Eventually I reserved a Tuesday morning flight, nonstop from O'Hare to Honolulu International Airport. With just a few clicks of the mouse, I had blown more than half of our budget. On top of that, I was already dreading being confined to a suspended metal tube for the equivalent of a work day. Still, it was the first tangible evidence (a la fat credit card bill) that we were actually going. Hooray... I think.

Knowing that the logistics of planning this trip would be my most complicated to date, I developed a plan to spread it out over the early months of 2013. Doing so, I believed, would divide up the bills as well as permit me to enjoy the mounting anticipation of, well, planning a trip to Hawai'i. Booking the flight, however, showed me that I wanted this trip researched, reserved, and checked off, from a planning perspective. I was not enjoying the process so much as conquering it.

The next week I sat down at the computer to tackle inter-island transportation. Surrounding me were my guidebook (a freebie rescued from the dumpster of the demolished bookstore), my credit card, maps of various

---

* a question upon which seemingly no experts agree

scales, myriad scribbled notes, and a pen that scratched out more notes than it kept. Early on in the discussions about going to Hawai'i, Senator and I had decided that we wanted to see Pearl Harbor, Hawai'i Volcanoes National Park, and any back country that did not involve other mainlanders. This would not be a trip of bikinis, umbrella drinks, and hotels, but a body/mind/spirit exploration of a place to which we would likely never have the opportunity to return. To do this required visiting a minimum of two islands: Hawai'i (also known as the Big Island) and Oahu. To afford this meant visiting a maximum of two islands.

I learned that in recent years, due to recession, all of the reputable inter-island boat services had either gone out of business or turned their attentions to more profitable ventures. There went that plan. In their place, two airlines offered convenient service to all of the main islands. I researched each. One sounded like it might be a small miracle if no mid-flight mishaps took place. The other boasted the safest record in the industry. I deemed our lives worth the extra fifty bucks and chose Hawaiian Airlines*.

The airline was chosen, but when and from where would we fly? This required finalizing the itinerary, which I could not do until I knew where we would be staying, which I could not know until I knew which days we would be on which island. (You begin to see the circular madness involved.) Everything depended upon everything else, which turned what should have been an enjoyable endeavor into a chore. Don't get me wrong, Reader. I don't

---

* Okay, so there are *some* exceptions to the apostrophe-in-Hawai'i rule.

mean to sound like a brat; I was very appreciative of the opportunity to go, and I was not complaining. I just started to feel a lot of pressure to coordinate so many factors.

I bit the bullet, decided which days we would do each activity, and booked inter-island flights based on that. It looked pretty doable on paper, and there was still time built in for other activities that might come up, so I declared it a mediocre success. My biggest concern was that we would be going to Pearl Harbor near the end of the trip. Well, so be it, but in case anything messed up the itinerary once we were there, I vowed not to leave Hawai'i until I had paid my respects at the Arizona Memorial.

So we had four flights set, which then required three different rental cars. I cringed at the thought of so much of our week being spent in airports and rental lines, but there was no other way to make it happen. In fact, "cringe" is a weak word. I hate, loathe, and detest renting vehicles. The companies are a short legal step above scam artists, the employees are generally suspicious of your intentions, the rates are outrageous, and the insurance parameters are unclear. Above all, there is the ubiquitous odd rental car smell.*

It was some consolation when I remembered that I had two different possibilities for discounts, either through

---

* Perhaps someone once smoked in the vehicle, which was then chemically purified with some questionable toxic concoction. Perhaps a child dropped his French fry under the passenger seat. Too encased in preservatives to decay, the errant spud fragment was content to take on a new indeterminate form. Perhaps it is simply the odor of corruption, as you are sure to find additional hidden charges somewhere on your bill if you are not careful.

my union or through my AAA membership. Both only worked for specific companies. Neither could match the rates of the cheapest one, which, naturally, is the one I chose. Three bookings later, I deducted the cost from our quickly dwindling Hawai'i budget. I left another line for the expensive gas we would have to purchases while there. Thus, the transportation outline was looking something like this:

    -drive to Chicago
    -flight #1 to Honolulu (Oahu)
    -rental car #1
    -flight #2 to Hilo (Big Island)
    -rental car #2
    -flight #3 back to Honolulu
    -rental car #3
    -flight #4 to Chicago
    -drive HOME

    I had my suspicions before, but now I was fully convinced. The trip to Hawai'i was proving itself to be more of a project to be accomplished, a feat to be achieved, than merely a vacation to be enjoyed. I had mixed feelings about that, but I was not dumb enough to look for anyone's sympathy. Once again I glanced at the budget, mentally grateful that we were taking an overnight flight home. That would save a night of lodging, which should just keep us within our targeted range. I put the file away for another week or so.

    It was still January, and I was still well ahead of schedule, but I was already sick of thinking about Hawai'i, if you can believe that. I just wanted the research and reservations to be done, so I could start dreaming about the freshest pineapple on Earth. Sometime around the middle of the month, I brought out the updated notes and dove into exploring lodging options. As I had on numerous occasions, I started looking for inns or bed and breakfasts. Normally, once I compile a decent list, I turn to my trusted travel review websites. From there I enlist Senator in the process of narrowing down the options according to our preferences.

  As it turned out, choosing lodging was the biggest headache of all. Though I knew which towns we wanted to stay in, my vision of quaint aloha-spirit accommodations was wavering. I learned that bed and breakfasts are rarely as well-maintained as on the mainland. In fact, I got the impression that many were illegally run, or too mismanaged and/or dirty. Simple I liked; dirty I would not pay for. *Heck, I can stay around my own mess for free.* Others were a bit too stingy with their online information, which was not the type of mystery I liked to dive into. Perhaps hotels were a safer bet.

  Then again, maybe not. After one frustrating two hour internet session with nothing to show for our efforts, Senator and I learned, to our mutual horror, that several of the hotels' patrons had reported roach sightings. The worst part was that these were nationally-respected chains... and not cheap ones. By early February, I was starting to get sick of Hawai'i, and I hadn't even been there yet. So far I knew it only as an expensive, dirty, buggy place. I was starting to think I needed to take this trip just to restore my faith in the decision to grant it statehood in 1959.

Within a few weeks I had (I hoped) successfully narrowed down choices of where to stay. In fact, after crossing off scary places, over-our-budget places, tourist purgatories, and everywhere else sketchy, the list was downright tiny. I made the necessary phone calls, approved the required deposits, and silently prayed that what awaited us at the other end of the phone line would not make me regret my decisions. Senator repeatedly tried to ease my mind, but I felt very unsure of our plans. I had taken risks before when outlining trips, but it seemed like this time was different. If things went wrong elsewhere, I suppose we always had a default backup plan. A chain of islands that sat 2,500 miles from the closest mainland however, was just so... inescapable. Well, there was nothing else to do except ignore it all for the next five months.

*   *   *

The spring proceeded as expected. Though Senator was no longer working retail, he was busier than ever. A week after his last day at the bookstore, his recording work shifted into high gear. The Chicago commute was becoming a regular part of each week, accented by a few trips to record in Milwaukee as well. Boredom was not part of our vocabulary.

Even when my summer school assignment ended, we found ourselves bouncing between late nights and more early mornings that we would have liked. Though we knew we were going to Hawai'i, we didn't have a moment to think about it, until about ten days before leaving. I preferred it that way. With the exception of a few nightmares about the lengthy plane trip*, I had successfully ignored my misgivings until it was practically time to pack. Actually, other people were anticipating it on our behalf more than we were. It almost seemed like a business task that just had to be processed.

It never really did set in, until our eyes popped open at 3:00am-- two hours before the alarm was supposed to go off. We were both aware that the other one was awake, but we both continued to pretend we were asleep. When it became clear that no one was getting any more rest, we got up and got ready. I tried to wrap my brain around the fact that by the end of the day I would be standing somewhere on that little sprinkle of dots far out into the Pacific. Hawai'i, one of two states that was always scrunched into the margin of U.S. maps like an afterthought, was our destination. I was stunned. I don't think I ever really believed it existed until that moment.

As we made our way to the car with our luggage, I noticed the bright full moon. It occurred to me that all my life I had easily looked up at a satellite that was millions of miles away, yet I could not see places just a few miles away. Space is funny like that, or I just needed to go back to bed for many more hours. We looked at our home, and bade the two raccoons we had startled in the back yard watch over it.

For the first time in years, we were on our way to O'Hare International Airport. That was unfortunate.

---

* most of which would be over water, which somehow (irrationally) made it seem worse

Normally we were able to avoid ORD*, but flying nine hours nonstop to Honolulu meant we had to use the 'big airport'. Almost anywhere but Chicago, Midway would be considered a very large airport, but next to O'Hare, it was a mere parking lot. And speaking of parking...

At this point, Reader, I would like to break for a brief public service announcement. Should you happen to have to park your vehicle at O'Hare, understand the way the lots work. First of all, know that the 's' at the end of lots was not a typo. When an airport serves a significant percentage of humans who fly, and it covers over 7,500 acres, there are many parking lots. Next, it is helpful to know the first seven letters of the English alphabet, preferably in their commonly established alphabetical order. Applying such knowledge will give you a mental image of your parking lot's relation to the terminals (again, not a typo). The earlier in the alphabet that your chosen parking lot's representative letter appears, the closer you are to somewhere that you will eventually need to be. Thus, A, B, and C place you a reasonable distance from transportation to the terminals. Parking in lot D or E requires a brisk hike to the transportation that will take you to the terminals, unless the shuttle comes for you, (which it surely will not). Should you fall prey to your budget-conscious side and opt for lot F or G, you might as well cancel your flight and look for Davenport brochures, as I believe these lots are located

---

* FAA abbreviation for O'Hare International Airport, which, for reasons unbeknownst to me, used to be called Orchard. I assure you that, as of at least July 2013, there is nothing resembling a fruit-bearing grove on this massive plot of land.

somewhere in Iowa.

We parked Roadie in Lot E, and I immediately wrote down the section, row, and paragraph numbers, just to make sure we would not spend years of our lives as nomads looking for our car upon our return. Just to be extra safe, I sketched a constellation map, referenced from the point of our parking spot. Senator unloaded our suitcases, locked up, and joined me for our sunrise trek to the monorail.

Growing up in Generation X, one is led to reasonably believe that the country will contain a vast network of monorails by the year 2000, (unless of course we are all living in outer space by then). Heck, Walt Disney saw it coming and rode that wave of the future right into Tomorrowland. Sadly, or maybe for the best, the monorail never saw its due recognition in the United States. That is, except at O'Hare, where millions of patrons rely on its single track people-moving powers.

With our luggage in tow, we joined the throngs of the bleary-eyed, ready to speed to our appropriate terminal. I held onto Senator, and he smiled at me. The first of many phases of transportation exchanges had been successful. I smiled back. After all, we were going to Hawai'i! I was starting to wake up and perk up, and not just because we were circumnavigating a massive airport while zipping along in an unmanned train.

The regular airport routines moved along without incident. Likewise, security was fine, even though I opted for the pat down over the human microwave. I have to say, despite all of the TSA horror stories of intrusive frisks of women in their 90s and frightened toddlers, my 'personal interview' went very smoothly. In each situation, a polite female agent asked me if I wanted to go to a private room, which I declined, preferring to stay around Senator and various potential witnesses. Then she carefully explained each step and why it was necessary, before using the back of her hands for the pat down. Honestly, I have had far more invasive physical contact while walking the halls of my high school as a teenager.

With the proper authorities satisfied that we were not on a mission to demolish the Hawai'ian Islands, Senator and I settled into some seats in the waiting area of our gate. As usual, we were far too early. When we became restless, we wandered around aimlessly, listening to the same security announcement approximately forty-two times. Half-hungry and half-bored, we proceeded to pay far too much for a crappy breakfast sandwich. (Cold egg on a processed croissant leaves much to be desired.)

Returning full circle, we plopped back down in our original seats. Even in an airport, people-watching can get old. I just wanted the flight over with. My mind wandered, and I suddenly had the thought that we would see someone we knew. Just then somebody called out. "Wendy? David? Oh my gosh!" I looked up to see a girl we had both worked with at the bookstore. Nicole was a friendly face from our early days together, and a welcome site among the sea of the nameless. I learned that she and her family would be on the same plane as us. I chose to take it as an omen of a good flight. Besides, we just found out that our flight would be ten minutes shorter than we thought. *Well, that's more like it!*

Thanks to the blessing of tranquil skies, a great staff, and some Jack Benny radio shows Senator had brought along, the flight sailed along easily. When we landed we were told that the weather was 90°F, humid, and "mostly cloudy". Looking out the window, that last part seemed inaccurate. It was then we learned that mostly cloudy meant still extremely sunny. Welcome to the true Deep South.

As we waited to file off the plane, I was filled with a sense of euphoria and satisfaction. Under the plane's wheels was the edge of Oahu. We had officially been to all fifty states. A lifelong goal of mine was accomplished, which is a rare and special moment for anyone. I think that excited me more than the fact that we had just arrived in paradise. Senator hugged me, and I beamed. In some ways, it was more meaningful to me than completing college.[*]

We exited the plane and entered the airport. To dispel any myths, no one greets you with a fresh floral lei when you arrive. Of course, for a fee, you can give yourself one; just visit the kiosk near the baggage claim. Once we had our luggage, we started to search for our car rental company's desk. Naturally, we found every company but the one we needed. Finally someone explained that we would have to catch their shuttle outside the nearby exit. *Good to know.*

After a while, the Dollar shuttle arrived. Our driver smiled and greeted us. He seemed genuinely content with

---

[*] (Go back and read the introduction that you skipped.)

his job. On the other hand, maybe he was just smirking, knowing that we were about to be deposited into a half-hour line. The desk clerk did not even bother to put up any pretense on behalf of the 'Aloha spirit'. He processed our reservation-- which, by the way, never saves time-- begrudgingly.

Normally when renting a car, the agent and renter do a visual inspection together. When he handed us our papers without mentioning it, I asked about it. He snapped back at me. "Yeah, we *know* about it. We already inspected it!" We were too hot and tired to argue, so we took possession of the vehicle, noting carefully the positions of scrapes and scratches. *Mahalo for nothin', Pal.*

During daylight savings time, Hawai'i is five hours earlier than Illinois. This fact, coupled with a long plane ride and an early morning, led me to plan absolutely nothing for our first night in the islands. Our only task was to find our hotel, grab something to eat, and go to bed. Woo-hoo! Tropical dream life!

Although, just navigating Honolulu streets can be its own adventure. It's not that they are laid out in a difficult pattern; they simply fail to distinguish themselves by name. It probably does not help that the native Hawai'ian language has only twelve letters*, almost half of which are vowels. When it comes to naming streets, city officials are apparently partial to H, K, and A. Even though I had good maps, I learned all too late that I tend to rely on merely the impression of a name when developing a visual map. For

---

*   A, E, H, I, K, L, M, N, O, P, U, W   Imagine it-- Hawai'ian *Wheel of Fortune...*

example, at home I might take Main to Jefferson to 2nd to Beecher. In my mind, these are all distinct, and if I happen to think 'Beaker' instead of 'Beecher', no harm done. Honolulu demands more specificity. You had better be exact when your route takes you from Kalakaua to Kalaimoku to Kuhio to Nohonani.*

Street names notwithstanding, we found our Waikiki hotel and parked in its garage. If you have learned anything about us or our interests in this series, you have likely just spit out your coffee in a wide impromptu spray across your easy chair. Waikiki?! Yes, you read correctly. I booked our first night at tourism ground zero only because we would be flying out of the same area the next morning. In case you are unfamiliar with Waikiki, think Vegas with less lights, no quality live shows, and the ocean on one side. Although, you cannot really see the ocean unless you are on the backside of one of the many resorts that lay claim to each span of the beach. In fact, I find it mind-boggling that, of all of the beautiful scenery in Hawai'i, the one stupid shot that ends up on most of the postcards is of Waikiki Beach, complete with congested line of hotels. I could rant on my distaste for Waikiki for many more pages, but I will sum it up in the words I shared with Senator. "God must have had fun making Hawai'i... and the devil must have had fun ruining Waikiki."

We soon settled into our hotel, which for economy's sake was about three blocks from the ocean. As a sort of consolation prize, we could see the Ala Wai Canal out our

---

* This was part of our actual route; no names were changed to protect the consonantally-challenged.

window. The room was reasonably clean, quite spacious, and even more pink. I do not mean 'dusty rose' or 'blush' or 'velvet sunset'; I'm talking more along the line of 'Pepto puke'. Just in case the paint color didn't set the intended mood, the 1960s textured wallpaper underscored it in the exact same hue. At least most of the time we would spend there we would have our eyes closed.

After a quick refresher, we decided to scout out some dinner. It was an easy, if not scenic, walk to the big action, so we left the car and headed toward the busier streets. Every expected tourist trap crap store was dutifully manned by sellers hoping to convince some googly-eyed Dakotan that she desperately needed an odd cloth wrap/skirt/towel/shirt thing. We strolled past plastic leis, wooden leis, shell leis, and even a few made of flowers. Dinner options for vegetarians in Honolulu are as follows: 1. veggie burger; 2. shave ice*. Everything else is derived from the sea (rightly so), or from pigs (of which there are plenty, thanks to Captain James Cook). After a long flight, we needed a little more than frozen water and syrup, so we walked into an outdoor tiki bar and ordered veggie burgers.

Ah, paradise. The venue was sectioned off from the main stream of tourist shoppers by a tiki fence, beladen with LED lights which chased each other in an attempt at a 21st century faux raindrop effect. Behind the bar a fan was aimed upward, blowing red and orange fabric in front of a red light, an ever-present reminder that we were in the land

---

* I know; you would think there would be a 'd' at the end of 'shave', but nope.

of the volcanoes. Finally, in case we still weren't convinced that we had arrived in America's Eden, a lounge singer and his karaoke machine did his best to entertain the crowd with such traditional Hawai'ian tunes as *Sweet Home Alabama, Oh, Pretty Woman, Lean on Me,* and *The House of the Rising Sun.* As an amateur interior decorator, I dubbed it all 'tiki-tacky'.

After dinner we decided to take a short walk, so at least the entire day would not be a waste. Since the beach was occupied by various signs claiming it for the hotels that lined it, we strolled along the quieter canal. Some large unusual brown fish with crazy big eyes followed us near the edge of the sea wall, seemingly happy for a little attention. We found a bench and sat to look at the hills in the backdrop. Technically they were very low mountains. As we chatted, two teams paddled outrigger canoes. It looked like they were preparing for a race.

I was glad we were in Hawai'i, but I was also glad we were getting out of Honolulu in the morning. I leaned my head against Senator as we noticed our first Hawai'i rainbow. When the rainbow faded, we picked ourselves up to walk the few blocks back to the hotel. We were both beat and ready to retire for the night. After all, it was already 6:30pm.

* * *

Wednesday morning I popped up at an inconvenient 2:30am. Despite the darkness and the fact that it was only 7:30am at home, I could not fall back asleep. By 3:00am I gave up and turned on the television. Fortunately, I discovered the Scenic Hawai'i channel, where one can watch endless hours of what paradise should look like. This worked out well since no sound was necessary as the camera zoomed over remote waterfalls, lush green valleys, and even a herd of wild gazelle-like creatures running in the back country. Senator slept on, missing the next segment, which mainly focused on creatively-presented meat. Most dishes featured tails.

When it came time to get up, Senator rose for his morning routine, while I dressed in front of scenic Hawai'i. I was now fully engrossed. Actually, I would recommend that if you ever have to spend all of a Hawai'ian vacation in Waikiki, you simply stay indoors with the t.v. tuned to this channel. You will leave far more satisfied.

Since I did not have to spend the entire week in Waikiki, I eagerly turned off the t.v. as soon as Senator was ready. We checked out and proceeded to the car return by following a series of streets involving Ks, Hs, Ns, and a healthy dose of vowels. Right on cue, the shuttle picked us up to take us to the airport. Our driver was a lot of fun. Her thick, curly black hair swayed and her corpulent body jiggled with every sharp turn and bounce of the van. Like a true Hawai'ian, she ended every other sentence with "Yeah?"*

She continued to talk to us until she had to radio about some unexpected construction near the airport. Grabbing the c.b., she informed her boss, "But I'm not gettin' on the freeway again. I'm already at the airport,

---

* The Hawai'ian *yeah* is much like the Canadian *eh*, or the French *d'accord*. It is used to ask for approval, to request solidarity in thought, or simply as ending punctuation.

yeah?" Shaking her head at the quickly-mounting traffic mess, she chuckled. "They gonna' have a lot of fun today!"

We had beat the rush hour, thankfully. We had plenty of time to check-in, get through security, and grab the worst eggs I have ever eaten. Let's just say the Chinese have not mastered the art of the American breakfast. Sprouts in cold eggs do not an omelet make, and microwaved brown n' serve rolls cannot convincingly be disguised as French toast. Still, the view of the sunrise on the mountains in the background and the exotic birds hopping around beautiful large flowers in the foreground were gorgeous.

Hawaiian Airlines is a small line, running from the islands to the mainland, but more often between the islands. It was a disappointment not to sail between the islands, but it was breathtaking to see them from above. I can now vouch for the fact that the water near the shore really does range from a stunning turquoise to deep sapphire. Further out, the caps of the waves look like frozen white speckles.

As we were admiring the view, the flight attendants, who wore floral shirts and tucked plumeria into their hair, came around and offered us our choice of local canned juices. We politely declined when I noticed that the "100% Hawai'ian juice" was 100% Hawai'ian, rather than 100% juice. Mainly it contained the same high fructose corn syrup as the pop at home. Oh well. We would find some real fruit later.

In less than an hour we had flown over the main chain of the islands. Heading southeast from Oahu, we had arrived on Hawai'i, or the Big Island. It was such a big island that it looked like the mainland from the air. Though it is by far the largest of the Hawai'ian Islands, it is fairly sparsely populated. As one person explained to us, "There are 1.3 million residents in Hawai'i. 1,000,000 of them live on Oahu." Enough said; it was good to be on Hawai'i Island.

We landed smoothly at the very small airport in Hilo. It was a short walk through the terminal to the outdoor breezeway that contained the car rental booths. There was no one else in line, and a friendly attendant checked us in easily and gave us the key to rental car #2. I was expecting to have to walk to a distant lot, but she casually motioned to the space behind her booth. In a parking lot about the size of those in strip malls were reserved about eight spaces for the company's cars. What a difference from the attitudes at the Honolulu branch.

It was about lunchtime, but we wasted no time eating. We drove the main two-lane road from Hilo to Volcano toward Hawai'i Volcanoes National Park. Though the drive only takes about forty minutes, it gradually climbs from sea level to about 4,000 feet. This meant that it also dropped 18°F, which made it just about perfect hiking weather. We had left the beaches and entered the rainforest.[*]

We parked the car at the visitor center just in time to join a ranger-led hike that was beginning. We didn't know what we were doing or where we were going, but if the few

---

[*] I loved the idea that we had to pack jeans, sweatshirts, and hiking boots to go to a tropical island. (I told you we were weird.)

kids on the tour could handle it, so could we. Our guide was very informative and entertaining. He showed us many exotic specimens of flora, including the invasive but brilliant bright, spiky, yellow wild ginger, with its red bursting centers. Attributed to a myth involving lost love, the flowers of another tree change color. Yet another plant literally stops breathing if the air quality is bad, which it sometimes is at the top of an active volcano. My favorite strange plant was an innocent-looking ground cover. We were warned that it was as sharp as broken glass, so no one touched it. Gently running your shoe or a stick over it, however, caused it to immediately recoil and close up. In just a second or two it changed from a wide, matted weed to just a few thin connected sprigs.

  The ranger also told us that the island had two critter problems: feral pigs and mongooses.* (Lest you be deterred from visiting the Big Island, I will note that we saw neither animal during our few days there.) The pigs have been a problem for decades, tearing through fields and becoming a general nuisance. Even though they are hunted for their meat, the population thrives.

  The mongooses serve as a monument to failed human planning and research. In the 19th century, as the sugar cane plantations grew in size and popularity, rats were attracted to their sweetness. To keep these pests out, someone had the bright idea to import the mongoose, a natural enemy of the rat. That same person or group of

---

* Though the subject is up for some debate, 'mongooses' is generally the accepted plural of 'mongoose', although 'mongeese' is not out of the question.

people never stopped to consider the fact that mongooses run about by day, whereas rats are nocturnal. Thus, they have coexisted peacefully and counterproductively for years.

The last stop on our tour with the ranger yielded a view we had never experienced before. We were at the rim of a wide crater, maybe a few miles across and a thousand or so feet deep. The bottom looked like black ash, and people were walking across parts of it. In the distance, one part of the crater floor served as the rim for a deeper pit, which looked to be about 1½ miles in diameter. This hole continually blew up plumes of whitish-gray smoke. It was the Kilauea Caldera. At its bottom, which was visible only from the air, was a blazing lava lake. Wow. We were standing in view of an active volcano. Not too many of those in Illinois.

We tore ourselves away from the view, making a point to remember which path we had taken, so we could return. We wanted to hike more, but we needed some food first. Just a mile outside the park was the tiny town of Volcano. It consisted of residential areas, a few guest houses, a gas station or two, a few restaurants, and an art studio/gallery. We had no interest in the restaurants once we saw the art studio, or more precisely, its parking lot. There, in the midst of the land of seafood and pork, was parked a lunch wagon that specialized in homemade organic vegetarian dishes.

We might be the only people to travel to Hawai'i and rave about the enchiladas, but once we tried the locally-grown avocado, along with fresh cheese, black beans, and brown rice, we were hooked. New England temporarily faded from memory. *Maybe I could just paint and sculpt and make ugly clothing and live off of the lunch truck's creations*, I thought, as I shared a ginger-mint lemonade with Senator. It would only be a 5,000 mile adjustment to my dream.

We finished one of the best meals I had ever enjoyed outside of our kitchen and drove back to the park. Our next point of interest was the Thurston Lava Tube. A lava tube, as you might guess, is the open tunnel left after hot lava has rushed through underground. Since it did not cool at that point, the result is a hollowed-out cave with glistening black walls.

Thurston Lava Tube is a popular attraction, partly because, well, it is a tube that was once filled with lava, and partly because it is a very easy walk from a parking lot. This makes it the prime destination of bus tours, senior citizens, and lazier tourists who want to pretend they 'walked the volcano'. As such, we had to park further away, and walk a half mile path to the main lot. Along that path, we accidentally stumbled upon the main trailhead that led to the bottom of the crater. Ah, we had discovered how all those tiny people we saw from the rim had found their way to the bottom.

It was a steep trail, with lots of switchbacks amid the thick rainforest growth. Though we were near the edge, as opposed to deep within a jungle, I wondered if we would encounter any tropical snakes. I wasn't about to miss this trek, but I kept my eyes peeled, just in case. It was only about 60°F outside, but we were starting to sweat. It was a good workout with a satisfying reward.

At the bottom we freely roamed the cracked black earth. Some of it consisted of large, sharp rocks, while other parts had more of a sandy texture. Most amazing were the trees that sprouted up randomly amid the onyx barren landscape. They were always alone-- about twenty feet from any other tree-- and stood about six to ten feet tall. Their round, glossy leaves seemed to be getting plenty of water from either rain or the atmosphere, but I could see no soft ground in which they could have established roots. As if to prove their defiance, each tree bloomed with fire engine red flowers. It was especially striking against the black background. Enjoying the strange scenery, we tromped our way among the rocks for awhile, and then started back up the trail.

At the top of the trailhead, the stream of tourists showed no sign of letting up, so we filed in among them to walk down to the lava tube. While it was somewhat remarkable to walk where rushing lava once flowed, I'm glad that I did not pay extra for the experience. It amounted to a short cave that could easily be traversed in about two minutes. Of course, the event might take a little longer if you are not good at navigating around tourists whose eyes have not quite adjusted to the darkness. They can make interesting obstacles, particularly if they are trying to figure out how to use the flash on their new camera.

Walking back to the car, we could see the clouds gathering quickly. It soon started to sprinkle, which we found refreshing.* As the week progressed, we learned that

---

*   ...and, I suppose, appropriate, considering we were in a rainforest.

in Hawai'i it can easily rotate between rain and clear blue sky ten times a day. In fact, it did rain every day that we were in the islands, yet there were no interruptions to our plans. It seemed to be part of the daily cycle.

We had hiked about four miles, so we took a break and let the car do some work. For eighteen miles we rode down the side of Kilauea toward the ocean, along Chain of Craters Road. We made several stops to view older craters from earlier volcanic activity. Each time we got out of the car, it seemed to have grown windier. I suppose this was because we were on increasingly exposed terrain.

Eventually our winding descent took us out of the trees and into the barren country. I had always pictured a lava field as a wide swath of burned-out land coming down one side of a mountain, sort of like a black ski slope. In reality, lava fields go on in all directions, as far as the eye can see, for miles and miles. In terms of stark monotony, it was the closest thing I had ever seen to the vast landscapes of the Sahara. Instead of sand, however, the ground was made of ropy mounds of hardened black toothpaste. Other parts resembled giant fields of crumbled Oreo cookies. We were in no way prepared for the immensity of it. The only reminder that we were still on Earth was the occasional view of the dark blue ocean on the horizon, depending on the direction in which the road was winding.

Chain of Craters Road eventually becomes a dead end. In case you get lost, you will know the road has ended because the highway will suddenly be interrupted by six foot-thick mounds of cooled black lava that overtook it when the current eruption began, back in 1983. In fact, it is what scientists recognize as the newest land on Earth. Just in case you are still unclear as to your route, there is a sign that says "ROAD CLOSED", forever frozen at an angle in the pahoehoe*. It is a poignant reminder of both the power of a volcano and God's sense of humor.

After climbing the lava roadblock for about a half hour, we walked the long, hot stretch of road back to the car. Before we left though, we took a very short walk to the edge of the island. There, due to the extremely high wind gusts, the sea was slamming into a natural rock wall. We leaned against the wall for a close view of the sapphire waves rolling in below. Some reached as high as thirty feet, and each one shook the rock like a rumble of thunder. The convergence of so many raw and powerful forces of nature was an awesome site. It was a great spot for just being.

When we could finally bring ourselves to leave the shoreline, we walked back to the car and drove up into the higher elevations again. Chain of Craters Road took us back into the park, where we made a quick stop at the visitor center. If we played our timing right, we could come back to see the real spectacle of the park later on that night. In the meantime, we drove into the secluded neighborhood to find lodging #2 of the trip.

So far it looked promising; there was thick foliage everywhere, anchored by giant leaves and well-kept, if small, properties. We soon found the one for which we had a reservation. *Okay, at least I did not book a place that did not*

---

* Pahoehoe (*puh-HOI-HOI*) is the ropy, smooth, frosting-like cooled lava, formed as such due to a slower flow velocity. Contrasting it is aa (*ah-ah*), the glassy, sharp cooled lava formed by faster flow.

actually exist. Like the other homes in the area, it had a casual feel to it, accented by lots of flowers that were in no danger of drying out. We parked the car in the front and went inside to register.

At first no one noticed that we were there, and we could not find anyone around. Against one of the older local customs, we left our shoes on, hoping we were not offending anyone. Eventually a host-- in his shoes-- greeted us from the kitchen. He was an easy-going guy who managed the home for the owner, who was not on the island. He gave us the tour and showed us our room.

Off the bedroom was a tiny lanai that overlooked a private, prehistoric-looking garden. More oversized leaves and flowers dripped from the latest shower, creating a cool, peaceful effect. He showed us how to use the electric heater-- a necessary item at that elevation, even in Hawai'i. He wrapped up his welcome with a few facts about the state. For all practical purposes, there are no snakes in Hawai'i.[*] *Hooray!* Mosquitoes are also almost unheard of, even in the rainforest regions. *Double hooray!* Maybe there was something to this paradise bit after all. Mauna Kea was regularly snow-capped. Though over six times the size of Oahu, the Big Island had less than 20% of Oahu's population. Though we might never return to Hawai'i, if we did, we knew which island would be our destination.

We took some time to clean up and relax before

---

[*] Though this is not technically true, there are no native snakes that anyone could expect to encounter, even while hiking. There is supposedly one species that even scientists have a hard time locating, as well as a few snakes illegally smuggled in, which again are extremely rare.

leaving again. Then it was off to sort through the scant dinner options. We were disappointed to find that the veggie truck had closed down for the day, but we were pleased to find a Thai restaurant open. Again, we could not fathom how a town of 2,500 people could support such a restaurant, yet at home a town of 150,000 could not keep a Thai place open to save its culinary reputation.

As we pulled into the parking lot, there was a thick fog rolling in. Something between heavy mist and light rain had also begun, and the car thermometer read 58°F. Ah, the tropics. You never see this side of Hawai'i in the guide books, but it was much more interesting than the sunny-and-88°F stuff.

We entered the restaurant. It was busy, but we were seated right away. The warm dining room was filled with the smell of sautéed veggies. We ordered something involving those veggies and pineapple. This was not just any pineapple; it was the first pineapple we had ever tasted before it had traveled thousands of miles to our grocery store. As a connoisseur of citrus, I can tell you that the fruit in my stir fry had such an intensely sweet, rich flavor, that tasting it can only be described as crawling into a pineapple, licking the intoxicating walls, and then falling into a very deep, pineappley sleep. Good night.

After dinner we drove out into the rain, turning down the very dark road that led to the national park. Though it was mostly cloudy, we could see far more stars than in even the rural areas at home. The Milky Way was vivid. I had almost forgotten about that. Shooting stars streaked occasionally.

Several miles later, we reached the end of the road and the summit of Kilauea. As Senator pulled into the crowded parking lot, we could see a vibrant orange glow to the south. A short path led us to the caldera overlook, and suddenly we were in a movie. The orange glow that lit up the otherwise black sky was the light coming from the pool of lava deep in the pit. During the day we had seen the billowing smoke, but this was far more dramatic. Though we could not see the lava itself, the inferno's aura was a vivid reminder that we were at the edge of an active volcano. It would have made a perfect backdrop for any number of horror plots.

Having hiked down into a crater, walked through a lava tube, climbed pahoehoe, and witnessed Madam Pele's[*] fire, we were ready to collapse for the day. We drove back to our room, still amazed at what we had seen. Inside, we kicked off our shoes and got ready for bed. It was only 9:00pm, but it felt closer to Chicago's time of 2:00am. Satisfied at the day's events, I clicked up the heater a notch or two, kissed Senator, and fell asleep immediately.

*   *   *

---

[*] In Hawai'ian mythology, Pele is the volcano goddess, or the goddess of fire. Like most mythological goddesses, Pele was mysterious, temperamental, and passionate. She also had trouble finding her own man. As such, she arrived in Hawai'i as a result of being chased by her sister, whose husband she had seduced. As her sister (who happened, ironically, to be the goddess of the sea) flooded out several of her attempts at homesteads, Pele eventually settled high up on Mauna Loa, out of the flood zone. Since then, she has spent most of her time feuding with other mythological characters, sending trails of lava down the mountain to the ocean, adding new land to the island, and occasionally harassing the mortals.

Still on a maladjusted sleep schedule, I woke up on Thursday at 4:00am. As it turns out, I *can* be a morning person; I just have to keep moving five time zones west. Not wanting to wake Senator, I laid around for an hour and mentally planned out our day. By that time he was awake too, so we decided on a pre-breakfast trip up the mountain to see the sun rise.

As long as I have known Senator, he has been the type of person who strongly values his morning shower before tackling the day's events. He feels better, thinks better, and works better once he's gone through this daily rite. Since it was still dark, he had time to slip into the shower before sun-up. "Aw no!" came the yell from the bathroom. 5:00am is not a pleasant time to find out there is no hot water. We were aware that the system might need regenerating, so he agreed to forgo the shower and try again after our ride. Disappointed but flexible, he dried off and put on warm clothes.

Soon we were in the car with the heat on, climbing our way up the only road to the top of Kilauea. The much higher Mauna Loa and Mauna Kea formed the backdrop to the north. In what seemed like a faster process than at home, the sun joined us, spreading pink, lavender, and light orange hues down the side of the mountains. It reminded me of melting sherbet. Also drifting down, just a step behind the line of sunlight, was a layer of clouds encircling Mauna Loa. While all of this was going on, a menacing storm cloud line was forming in the east. I caught myself automatically scanning the sky for any funnel clouds before remembering that I was nowhere near tornado alley.

When the sun was fully risen, and the colors were starting to fade, we left. Fifteen minutes later, Senator was stepping back into the shower, praying for hot water. There were no promising signs. It was impossible that the hot water could have run out, since no one else was up to use it. We had also given the reservoir tank plenty of time to reset. Running short on time, we noticed that the room next to ours was vacant. Senator stealthily used that shower, wiped it down, and came back to our room.

We planned to talk to the host as soon as he was done serving breakfast. For the moment, though, there were more pressing matters at hand, like sampling local fresh fruit. On our plates were ripe papaya boats with juicy pineapple and blueberries. Looking over my options, I chose to spread my bagel with guava jelly. To this day I cannot tell you exactly what a guava is, but I can tell you it is delicious when mashed with cream cheese.

Our innkeeper was winding down his work, and we were finishing our coffee, so it seemed like a good time to approach him with our dilemma. "Ah," he began knowingly, "It's been acting up the past few days. We have hot water 'on demand' here. I can reset it for you."

"We figures something like that," added Senator, "because we were 'demanding' but it wasn't responding." He followed the host outside to a small box on the side of the house. Senator, to his credit, decided to learn for himself how to fix it, in case we ran into further trouble. With the problem easily solved, we resumed our routines and left to go hiking for the day.

Months before, as I prepared a list of hiking options, I made notes next to each trail. Some looked very promising, while others looked a bit out of our (or more accurately, my) range of ability, or at least comfort. Next to the Iliahi Trail, I had written "probably not", due to its warning to "Beware cliffs, cracks in crust, and scalding steam vents". Naturally, when I happened to mention this to Senator, he jumped on it as the trail that we were destined to conquer. I should have known.

The trailhead was a little obscured, but once we found it, it was a rolling path into the cool rainforest. Some areas were so thick that it was heavily shaded. Around certain bends we could see the deep crater in the distance, endlessly pouring out smoke. We had to be careful in a few spots, mainly due to the possibility of slipping over steep drops, but one would have to be pretty careless to have had that happen. Cliffs and cracks mastered, we wondered if we would encounter any scalding steam vents.

Just then, Senator, who was trailblazing in front, stopped abruptly because his glasses had immediately fogged over. A half-second after he started to tell me, I was startled by entering an instant sauna. "The steam vents!" I yelled, utilizing my brilliant inductive reasoning skills. We looked over the side of a small natural bridge and saw steam pouring out of a hole. The wind carried it gently over just enough to cross our path. It was a strange sensation, though thankfully, not one of being scalded.

We encountered several more steam vents along the sides of the trail. It was odd to think that these holes, just a few feet in diameter, eventually led to volcanic activity far below. It is in part because of the steam vents that Mount Kilauea is so accessible. The vents let off pressure, so that eruptions are more gradual, and they tend to give plenty of warning ahead of time. How very convenient.

Having survived all potential peril on the Iliahi ridge, we walked to the visitor center for a short break and the requisite visitor center video. This one lasted thirty minutes and was filmed in that zealous documentary style that can only come from the 1950s. *...From the people who brought you "Duck and Cover"...* Using overenthusiastic narration, the film spouted as much information as lava. It was like reading an encyclopedia with the visual of the Earth hurling its guts in the background.

1950s Voiceover Guy went on to tell us how important-- though dangerous-- it was to gather data during an eruption. At that point the footage showed two scientists setting up their equipment right next to the violently spewing lava and ash. I don't remember many of the statistics that we were supposed to learn, but apparently the proper protective gear when working in such hazardous SO_2 conditions consists merely of J.C. Penney casual wear and a floppy cotton hiking hat. As Senator pointed out, all the man was missing was a Lucky Strike cigarette. Frankly, after a half hour of watching various eruptions from every conceivable angle, I was rooting for the volcano.

Our final jaunt through the national park was on Devastation Trail.* It was only a half mile walk, on a level trail. Its impact lay in the fact that it followed the border

---

* If I ever start a metal band, I may borrow this name.

between lush growth and barren volcanic ground. One side was alive with native plants and birds. The other was a black field with only a sprig or two of determined plant life. At the dead end a fence protected onlookers from sliding down the eroding edge as they surveyed the wasteland, some of which was still warm from a 1959 eruption. Needless to say, we obeyed the sign forbidding hikers from going further.

Our time on the Big Island was limited, so we made another lunch stop at the wondrous veggie wagon and then departed to the shore. In Hawai'i there are four colors of sand (yellow, white, black, and green) depending which beaches you visit. While green would have been interesting, the idea of a black beach was too irresistible to pass up. Over the mountain we rode, listening to a cd of Hawai'ian folklore on the way.

Upon reaching the entrance to the beach, we could see dozens of people picnicking, playing at the water's edge, and cooking out. A five minute walk took us to a secluded lava rock embankment, so we quickly evaded the crowd. The sky was mostly overcast, but the wild, high waves were still a deep blue, all the way from their origin out in the ocean until the moment their white tops broke and crashed into the beach. Fog was rolling down the mountain behind us. We were on a black beach in jeans and long sleeves. This was a Hawai'i I could go for!

The tide was coming in fast, creating swirling pools and bringing fish to new temporarily homes. We moved in for a closer look. Every time my attention shifted to the shallow pools however, I was again distracted by the massive force of the oncoming waves. I was reminded of an early verse in the Bible, where it talks about the Spirit of God "moving upon the face of the waters".* It was humbling.

As I was meditating on the scene, something caught the corner of my eye. I looked, but I could not see anything but the chunky black lava rock. Then I saw movement again. I called Senator and we examined the rock more carefully. Every time the tide washed back out, dozens of jet-black crabs scrambled their way upward. When they saw us, they froze and were soon washed down again. They would have been kind of creepy if they weren't so fascinating. These guys certainly did not make it into any of the travel brochures I had read.

We sat together in the wind and let the salt spray us until the rain became strong enough to chase us back to the car. I had heard of sunny Hawai'i and blue Hawai'i, but I was really falling for gray Hawai'i. All we needed to complete our afternoon was a cup of Kona coffee. Back up the mountain we went.

We had been talking for months about finding a coffee shack along the road. Our fantasy included a native Hawai'ian whose family had harvested and roasted beans for six generations. He would smile when he handed us our paper cups in exchange for cash, (the only medium in which he dealt). Then we would toast each other, kiss, and proceed to burn our tongues due to impatience.

It was a lovely dream, but not at all accurate. Though we did find two rustic coffee stands, one was

---
* Genesis 1:2

abandoned, and the other looked too shady. Actually, what we were seeing in the rural areas reminded us of the reservations in the western states, right down to the scraggly stray dogs that ran around the streets. Sadly, Hawai'i has a disproportionate amount of poverty, and much of the housing is cramped and run-down. As we assumed, Waikiki is not the real Hawai'i.

We drove on, stopping only twice while crossing to another part of the island. First we gassed up the car, and later we paused for a coffee shack that was just about to close. We each ordered a cup at the counter, and unenthusiastically accepted the warmed over liquid in the styrofoam cup. I made a mental note to congratulate myself on not bothering to book a tour through the coffee plantations.

Coffee or not, we were on a mission. Earlier in the day, while at the visitor center, the updated memo board showed a road that led to where the lava still flowed. Kilauea has been erupting gradually in one spot or another since 1983, and thirty years later the trail supposedly spouted out of one of the lower foothills, smoking and running all the way down to the ocean, where it met the water in a splash of steam. We were eager to see this dynamic counterpart to the smoking caldera. Maps and directions in hand, we made the hour drive with plenty of time before sunset.

Everything was easy until we reached what would have, should have, and could have been the last mile or so. Our road ended, and not at any visible trail o' lava. The road we were on was barricaded and closed. I secretly hoped it was because the lava river had swelled to several times its width, but it was only due to construction.

Noting a side road that seemed to go in the same general direction, we decided to take that instead. We were somewhat encouraged to see a few other tourist cars going the same way, but I thought there would have been a sign, or a ranger station, or someone by the side of the road selling "I survived a VOLCANO!" tee shirts. Not so. That road also ended in a cul-de-sac, with only an ice cream parlor, a portable toilet, and a path of black boulders that led to the beach. No signs, no rangers, no lava.

In an impromptu family meeting, we unanimously determined that the beach would offer more scenic options than either the ice cream joint or the outhouse, so we started down that path. A wide flat area made it easy to see our way to the water's edge, which was about a half mile away. We still took our flashlight though, recognizing that once the sun set there would be very little light in such a remote area. That is, of course, unless we found fire trailing down the side of the mountain.

On we walked for about an hour. At one point a German man and his wife passed by. He informed us that he knew "awl about ze area" because he had been there twenty years earlier. He also made a point of telling us our flashlight was inferior, and that we had better stick with them. That confirmed it; we would definitely do this alone.

The sun continued to slip behind the mountain. With each deeper layer of twilight, I scanned the horizon in concentrated search of anything that looked like a line of smoke. A few times I thought I spotted something promising, only to realize that it was a layer of mist floating through. Powerful waves slapped the shore endlessly. At least we were getting to see the sun set on a Hawai'ian beach, but it was not how we had pictured our adventure. As the earliest stars twinkled in the sky, it became apparent that we were not to see any lava on this trip.

I couldn't help but think that maybe if we had just walked another twenty minutes or so... but Senator assured me that if there was any lava, it was miles away. Soon it became a safety decision to start back toward the car. The rocks we walked/climbed over were very black and very sharp. Like much of the newly formed earth, there were crevices that dropped down a few feet. A misplaced step in the dark could mean a horribly sprained ankle, one of us hobbling a mile back to the car, and spending the rest of the night looking for a hospital. Plus, I had to admit, the German was right about our lame little flashlight. Stupid lava.

By the time we got back to the car it was raining. The road looked very different on the way out, which resulted in us missing a turn and backtracking a few miles. Nothing was as creepy as the eerie sounds from the rural areas. They joined in a screech-humming chorus that would never exist in daylight. Someone later suggested that they were monkeys, but I have found no evidence to support that claim.* Disappointed, but dry and safe, we drove back to the bed and breakfast. We had been awake since before sunrise and spent the entire day hiking and roving around the outdoors. It was time for a shower and

---

* On the other hand, I have found no evidence to discredit that claim.

bed.

Back in our room, Senator kindly offered to let me have the shower first. With twelve hours' worth of sand, sweat, salt water, and sunscreen build-up, I was grateful. I stepped in, turned on the water, soaped up, and screamed. The hot water had gone out after just thirty seconds. Thankfully, Senator had the forethought to learn how to reboot the failing hot water system. Immediately he went outside, and in a few minutes he was back in the bathroom. "Fixed?" he asked hopefully. No such luck.

He continued to fight with the system. He called the host, but the man was unreachable. The host's nephew was staying upstairs, but he was unable to fix it either. Meanwhile I was gross, soapy, and shivering, naked in the shower. The entire house was booked, so we couldn't switch rooms. It was also too late to get a room elsewhere, not to mention the small matter of my freezing, naked, mid-shower self. I wondered how this would play out once everyone realized that there was no hot water. Then the nephew explained that only our shower, his apartment, and the kitchen sink were affected. That meant that we could not use his bathroom, however, we could get hot water out of our sink.

On to plan B. As I stood in the shower, Senator continuously dumped coffee cups filled with warm sink water over me. He then washed my hair in the sink. Between us, we spilled at least a quart of water on the floor. Then it was his turn. He opted for the more convenient but far colder option of a regular shower, sans heat. In return for his kindness, I cranked the heater on the bed and had warm pajamas ready for him the instant he was through, which was as quickly as possible. Highly annoyed, but grateful for the hot water of the sink, we fell asleep.

*   *   *

The next morning there was still no hot water. Again we waited for an opportune time to tell our host, who was busy wrapping up breakfast. Again he apologized profusely. It really was not his fault; he had notified the owner of the problem, and she had done nothing. I made a mental note to contact her when we got home. As two individuals who had decades of experience in customer service between us, Senator and I found the situation unacceptable.*

Even so, we were in a good mood and ready for our next adventure. We enjoyed more excellent fruit and checked out. Though we hated to leave the Big Island, we were eager to see other aspects of Hawai'i. Back down the two-lane mountain road we drove, headed for the airport.

We returned car #2 without incident, to the same

---

* For those interested in the outcome, once we were home, I contacted the owner via email and explained everything that had happened. Trying to be fair, I requested that she refund one night out of the two that we had stayed. I expected her-- as I would have done-- to trip over herself apologizing for the hassle, the wasted time, and my boyfriend's efforts to fix HER hot water system, but no dice. Not only did she refuse to credit any portion of the stay, but she actually called us liars. *Aloha spirit my ass!* We were dumbfounded. Unfortunately, it was out of the jurisdiction of our credit card company, so I was forced to seek justice via www.tripadvisor.com. It is the only scathing travel review I have written to date, and I sincerely hope she lost more business than the two nights' fees she made from us.

sweet lady from whom we had rented it. She was stationed in the same place with the same friendly smile. Glancing behind her, I still could not believe how small the rental car lot was. Although, considering that it took all of fifteen minutes to go through check-in, security, and our gate, I should not have been surprised. In fact, it was so smooth that we had lots of time to kill in the overgrown-living-room-of-a-terminal. We found seats among the oversized, comfortable chairs scattered among the koa wood coffee tables. The airport at Hilo was like no transportation hub I had ever seen.

Flight #3 was short, scenic, and enjoyable. Car rental #3 was another story. Upon being deposited at the same rental facility we had used for rental #1, we found ourselves crammed into the small building full of sweaty, long-suffering tourists. We wound our way back and forth along the line, occasionally attempting to suck in our guts for people trying to squeeze out. At one point, when we had conquered about half of the journey to the desk, a woman in the front of the line completed her paperwork and received her keys. She was so ecstatic after the long wait that she was cheering and beaming, announcing to all, "Yes, I finally got it!"

After shuffling through the ranks for an hour and a half, we finally earned our turn. At that point all I wanted was a set of keys that would get me the heck out of Honolulu. A shower would be welcome too, since the building was glass halfway around it, creating a lovely greenhouse effect for those trapped inside. I took out my papers and silently thanked God that we did not end up with the same snotty agent as before.

Senator loaded our gear into car #3 as I took my position as navigator, arranging the two crucial maps. He started up the car, and I reached over to crank up the air conditioner in the black exterior/black interior vehicle that had been baking in the sun in anticipation of our arrival. As I did, I noticed the gas gauge. It was only ¼ full, but we had been told it would be completely full. In other words, we could either eat the difference or be penalized when we returned it with the same quarter-full tank. After the miserable wait inside, there was no way we were going back. They had us. Thus, I submit this as further evidence that all car rental agencies are corrupt.

It was too late and we were too hot to start a hike at Diamond Head as originally planned, so we drove the half hour over the low mountains to the windward side of Oahu. Though a combined total of less than twenty-four hours had been spent in Honolulu on this trip, we were in agreement that it was too much. We were happy to check in to our guest apartment over the garage of one of the many modest homes dotting Kailua, on the opposite side of the island. The town was a bit bigger than I had pictured it, but it was a pleasantly buzzing community sandwiched between rounded mountain slopes and a long sand beach that has the reputation of being one of Hawai'i's cleanest and safest. As an added bonus, no condos swallowed it.

We rested a while at the apartment, (which, incidentally, had hot water during our entire stay). It was late Friday afternoon, and nothing in particular was on the agenda, so we decided to take a leisurely drive up the East

Coast. We still had hopes of stumbling upon a roadside coffee shack, or maybe a stand that sold fresh fruit. Even if these visions did not materialize, we would at least be guaranteed awesome scenery, since the entire road was a coastal highway.

    Just out of curiosity, what did you picture just now, Reader, when you read the phrase "coastal highway"? Me too. I envisioned a road with a steady view of the ocean in the not-too-far distance. I assumed it would probably resemble parts of California's PCH*. Highway 83 fulfilled this image. Mile after mile of shoreline views included scenes of surfers, swimmers, picnickers, and gentle waves rolling into offshore boulders. What set it apart, however, was the fact that it was so close to the water that the car was occasionally splashed by incoming waves. When the map of Highway 83 shows a red line following the edge of the island, believe it!

    Up the coast we continued, intermittently driving in rain and sun. Rainbows popped up here and there, fading quickly and, it seemed, eliciting no one's interest but ours. Because of so much water and light, they are a common occurrence in Hawai'i, as noted on their license plates.† What caught my attention even more than the rainbows was the fact that no one-- and I mean no one-- bothered to get out of the water when it started to rain. They never seemed to notice or care.

---

*   Pacific Coast Highway, or Highway 1

†   Yet another unique experience while driving in Hawai'i is the monotony of local license plates. Whether local or tourist, everyone is driving a car with Hawai'i plates. Think about it...

While there was plenty of natural beauty to behold, the drive took us past more of real Hawai'i. It was crowded, and we passed countless neighborhoods and trailer parks of run-down homes. Along some parts of beaches people camped, and the campsites looked a little too permanent. Lots of people seemed to just be hanging around. We did eventually find a stand that sold beautiful fresh fruit, but only after stopping at one or two that did not pan out-- read: roaches.

We continued back down the same road, reaching the apartment just as darkness set in. As you have probably figured out, trendy night clubs and tropical bars are not our scene, so we spent the rest of the evening planning the next day and sampling our local fruit. Results were as follows: pineapple-- so deeply sweet and rich that I and the fruit became one; dragon fruit-- gorgeous with its pink, spiky outside, but disappointingly bland inside; papaya-- divine, and depressing to think that real papaya is nowhere to be found on the mainland; guava-- good, but better as a jelly... on a bagel... with lots of cream cheese; and some little things that were surprisingly hard and bland. With our tummies full of our makeshift Hawai'ian buffet, we fell asleep, still hovering somewhere between Chicago and Honolulu time.

* * *

Saturday morning I woke up excited and nervous. For as long as I could remember, I had wanted to visit the site of the 1941 Pearl Harbor attack. If it had been anywhere closer than Hawai'i, I would have made it there several times by now, probably initially with my parents, who constantly went above and beyond the call of duty to take their kids to significant historical sites. Hawai'i is not on the way to anywhere save a few other islands and Asia, however, so I had waited a long time to see Pearl Harbor. The time was finally upon me.

  I was so antsy that I could not sit still. Half of me was superstitious that something would happen to prevent our going. If so, we had one backup day left, but there was the matter of tickets. The memorial was free, but reservations were recommended for time slots on the U.S.S. Arizona. In fact, I am such a realist that once I found out I could book our time slot up to six months in advance, I marked the important January date on the calendar and subsequently reserved early that morning. As I dressed in red, white, and blue, I obsessively checked the time (way early), the tickets (same date and time as the other fifty times I had checked), and the directions (two easy roads). There was plenty of time, but I still found myself eating too fast as we had a picnic breakfast outside a carry-out deli. We watched the sun climb higher in the sky, and I tried to imagine what I would see in just an hour or so.

  The first thing I saw upon entering the parking lot were the many signs warning us that we were in a "high theft area". Natives of the greater Chicago area, we were not naive enough to leave valuables in the car, but I was still surprised. After all, the memorial was only open during daylight hours, and there was a constant flow of visitors and staff members. It also occurred to me that a thief would have to be pretty determined, since the entire complex was still part of a military base. Apparently

Honolulu thieves are both bold and stupid. Consider yourself warned.

We stepped from the empty rental car into the bright sunlight. The black interior was sure to be toasty by the time we returned. As we entered the memorial campus, swift cool breezes drove the encroaching heat away, making it feel more like a dry day in May. Our first stop was the visitor center. Like other national visitor centers, it provided an excellent multimedia education. One hour in, I had an in-depth understanding of the U.S. and Japanese situations leading up to the attack, why the attack was so successful (initially)*, and how it impacted the locals and the rest of the country. Taunting me was the massive collection of primary source diaries, audio clips, and video interviews that was too numerous to tackle in full... not that it stopped me from trying.

We continued into a theatre that brought the details of that fateful day together into one human narrative.

---

* In a nutshell, there were a few key reasons that the attack was such a surprise to the United States, despite our expectation of trouble from Japan. For starters, peace talks were actually progressing smoothly. Our advanced radar also picked up the Japanese planes early on, however, we tragically ignored it since one of our own squadrons was due back at that time. Against some advice, top brass had also ordered U.S. planes lined up wingtip-to-wingtip in an open field, as a measure against sabotage by locals of Japanese descent. Once engaged, the Japanese effectively utilized their horizontally-oriented torpedoes, allowing them to cause mass devastation, even in the relatively shallow harbor. Perhaps most amazing of all was the fact that the Japanese carrier ships managed to travel 4,000 miles together with zero radio communication, allowing them to move undetected.

Interviews with both American and Japanese pilots were included, neither of which had forgotten any aspect of those moments that forever changed the war and the world's history. In the aftermath, almost 2,500 American and Allied lives were lost. It was gripping; I was barely aware of anyone else in the room, though I know there were about 100 others.

One thing that stood out especially in my mind was the plight of the local people. Even those born in Hawai'i and loyal to the United States were instantly treated as potential spies or traitors, based solely on race or ethnicity. Though one has to be careful sitting in judgment with the advantage of over seventy years of hindsight, some measures that were taken seem completely inappropriate. Hawai'i was immediately placed under temporary martial law, which is understandable, but President Roosevelt issued an act of Japanese containment, effectively imprisoning many innocent fellow Americans. Only time will tell if we have learned any useful lessons from our haste.

When the movie ended, it was time for one of the most meaningful moments of my life as a historian. With our carefully guarded six-month old tickets clutched in our hands, we left the theatre and boarded a Navy-operated tender boat for the ten-minute cruise out to the sunken U.S.S. Arizona. We could see its iconic white form gleaming out on the water. It resembled a floating hallway, with several open-air windows. Camera poised, we took our seats.

During the brief ride, we could see several other

battleships in the harbor. The scale can only be described as immense, dwarfing that of cruise ships I have seen. As we motored closer to the memorial, I felt the full weight of its somber presence. Standing so proud in the water bordering the beautiful islands, it was not so depressing as incredibly moving.

Carefully and quietly we all filed out of the boat onto the ramp leading up to the open air memorial. Instantly I was surrounded by the intense smell of engine oil. I cannot blame the phenomenon on power of suggestion; I had been thinking about the people, not the ships. Yet it was more pervasive than if I had been standing next to a fleet of vehicles. Call it eerie or call it a supernatural tribute or call me crazy, but I could smell it distinctly and strongly.

We were now poised perpendicularly over the center of the U.S.S. Arizona, sunk beneath us almost entirely. Only a few of its highest points peaked out above the water line. The memorial's walkway is not large, but it can accommodate perhaps several dozen people. Visitors are given twenty minutes or so to look around and talk to a guide.

At some point, most visitors look over the side of the center of the walkway. That is because, as we saw, the Arizona leaks oil to this day. The trickle has faithfully been oozing upward with no sign of stopping for the past seventy-two years, causing some to suggest that the ship still weeps for its crew and all of the others lost that day. The small puddle still did not account for what I had smelled, which was actually stronger further away from the leak. Regardless, I believe it is a consecrated place.

The end of the memorial culminates in a room with a tall, solid white stone wall. On it are engraved the names of those entombed in the harbor. There are also several blank spaces left. These wait patiently for the names of men who survived the attack and have chosen to exercise the honor of someday being buried in Pearl Harbor with their fellow veterans.

As we taxied back to the shoreline, I sat amazed, humbled, and grateful. I firmly believe we owe our lives and certainly our country's freedom to our military, and especially to those members of the Greatest Generation.* There was more to see, but I didn't think anything else during the trip could compare to that moment. I would soon find out that I was wrong.

We were done at the memorial complex, but not far away was the Pacific Aviation Museum. The previous January I had belabored the decision of whether or not to pop for tickets to the museum. I was sure it would be well done, and I held a somewhat genetic fascination with aviation history, but... twenty bucks was twenty bucks, and it seemed a little steep for a single admission. Canceling Hawai'i was non-negotiable, but we were still conscious of cutting corners wherever possible.

I brought the question to Senator, who makes these decisions far easier than I do. "Let's go! What are you even debating? If you want to go, we'll do it." I think I

---

* Although, I recently heard someone say that the Greatest Generation was *not* the greatest. Rather, it was their parents who raised them with the strong values, determination, duty, and gratitude that drove them to persevere in the most demanding times.

eventually rationalized the ticket purchase as an investment in my career as a history teacher. I somehow classified it as a job duty. To heck with frugality; I was about to see a Japanese Zero!

Thus, we found ourselves on the shuttle bus to Ford Island. On the way, we passed the "Mighty Mo" (otherwise known as the U.S.S. Missouri), where the Japanese had signed the surrender to the United States. A recording on the bus gave us a little more information about what we were seeing. On the day of the attack, the entire island was surrounded. Now it mainly consists of military barracks. In at least one of the airplane hangars on the island, damage from the attack is still visible.

We soon pulled up to the entrance for the museum, and stepped down off our bus. Our visit started with another film. I think the statement of one American pilot in the movie best encapsulates the spirit of Pearl Harbor:

>"We were 19, 20 years old, and we just knew we had to do this. There was no question or debate. You were watching out for your buddy, and he was watching out for you, and so you went together..."

We exited the theatre and came around a curve to the main exhibit, housed in the entirety of the hangar. We were startled by an Asian-American pilot who was dressed in full Japanese uniform, standing by a Zero taken captive during that era. After spending a day immersed in a history that saw the rising sun as a threat, it was quite a striking site.

The museum boasted several other aircrafts of the

mid-20th century, including those of George Bush, Sr., Amelia Earhart, and an innovative Chinese pilot. We made the rounds and then followed the signs to the other hangar. There, we were told, we could view several more planes and helicopters. It sounded like an impressive collection, so by this time I had deemed the tickets officially worthy of their price.

Impressive it was. There were at least two dozen military fighter planes from the World War II, Korean War, and Vietnam War eras. We also had the chance to inspect a cut-away rescue helicopter and the exposed cockpit of what I think was a bomber. We climbed up for a close look at all of the complicated (yet primitive by today's standards) gauges and dials. The most significant site at that hangar, however, was not a plane.

Just inside the massive doors of the hangar was an elderly man sitting at a plain folding table. Sitting with him was a younger man who seemed to be assisting him. A box fan was cooling them both. Normally I would not have thought much about it, except for the modest sign that sat on the table. On a framed sheet of paper read the words that got this history lover's heart pounding: "Meet a Pearl Harbor Survivor-- DICK GIRACCO".

I could hardly believe the opportunity that stared me in the face. I was literally shaking. This was my meeting-a-rock-star moment, yet I wanted to maintain respect and dignity for this veteran who witnessed one of our darkest days firsthand. I took Senator to the side so we could plan a correct approach. He was interested, too. "The last thing I want to do is upset this man, but I assume there would not be a sign like that if he did not want to talk to people," I explained to Senator, who was nodding in agreement. "It's not like I am ever going to get a chance like this again..." I continued. Senator was already adjusting the camera settings to shoot brief video footage. "I think the way to start is just to first get his permission to film him. Then I could explain that I am a teacher, and just ask him what message he would like to give young seventeen and eighteen year old kids." Senator liked the idea because it gave Mr. Giracco an easy, open-ended question that did not necessarily corner him into speaking about that attack.

 Knees wobbling, I approached the table. There was no waiting; no one else had visited the table the entire time we were preparing our introduction. Nervously I introduced myself and Senator and explained our mission, asking the aforementioned question. His response about knocked us over. We were expecting a little bit of small talk, or maybe a 'stay in school, kids' type of statement, but he immediately went into every vivid detail of his memory of the Japanese attack.* I was awed, dumbstruck, and grateful beyond what my weak thank-yous could express. I tried to tell him what his service and willingness to talk meant to me, but I am sure I failed at fully conveying my appreciation.

 We shook hands with Mr. Giracco once more, and then turned to walk toward the last of the exhibits. There were a few planes outside that we still wanted to see on our way out of the hangar. Not fully believing that we had just experienced a personal interview with an eyewitness to the

---

*   (See Appendix A for full transcript)

Pearl Harbor attack, we looked over at the table one last time. The sign was gone, the fan was motionless, and no evidence remained to suggest that anyone had ever been there. I have never been so thankful for the ability to shoot video.

Back at the main complex, we saw the outside of the Bowfin, a World War II submarine better known as the "Pearl Harbor Avenger". Appropriately, the state-of-the-art stealth fighter was launched one year to the day after the Japanese attacked. It was stationed in Pearl Harbor, of course, and proudly stands there still. Although we did not tour the inside, visitors can do so for a fee.

Turning around from the Bowfin, we could see one other odd contraption. It looked like a long, black torpedo, and it was, of a sort. What made this artillery unique was the fact that it was a manned torpedo. The Japanese used the single-man weapon during the war, under the claim that the operator could escape through a roof hatch just before deployment. Of course, this rarely (perhaps once?) happened. Thus, they are commonly referred to as 'suicide torpedoes'.

We surveyed the Pearl Harbor grounds and shore one last time before walking to the car. We had made it to yet another significant memorial, adding it to a list that already contained Wounded Knee, Ground Zero, and a field in Shanksville, Pennsylvania. The hours at Pearl Harbor were worth all of the planning, expense, headaches, and even lack of hot water associated with the trip. I truly encourage anyone who can do so to visit these sites. It may impact your ideas about freedom for the rest of your life.

Upon arriving at our very hot, black vehicle, I was happy to find it intact, with all of our valuables (maps, pen, handwritten directions) safely inside. As a fitting end to our excursion, we decided to drive up to the Punchbowl, an extinct crater that is now the site of the National Memorial Cemetery of the Pacific. As with the rest of Hawai'i, the street names contained mostly vowels, with a few Ks, Hs, and Ls for good measure. As with the rest of Honolulu, the street names changed at will, and did not necessarily connect the way they did on my map. Since there was no grid layout, and we were driving in a continuous curve as we tried to find a route up to the top of the crater, it took several attempts.

Eventually we reached the top. There we entered what I had expected to be a bigger graveyard, but it was stately nonetheless. A large monument was the focal point, situated at the rear of the cemetery, where several roads converged. Locals flowers were on many graves, and one side of the 'bowl' spanned a wide view of the bay. In the background were dense neighborhoods built into the foothills.

We meandered for a while, but soon we were ready to head back to our apartment. It was a lot to take in for one day. In fact, it was a lot to take in for one trip. The rest of the evening was devoted to relaxing, reflecting, reasoning... and then watching a campy black and white movie on cable*. Hey, it's all about balance, right?

---

* 1962's *Wild Guitar*, starring Arch Hall, Jr. as a naive singer/songwriter who makes it big, only to learn that sometimes-- just sometimes-- record executives are not always pals looking out

*   *   *

Sunday morning I was up too early again. By this point I had given up on any sane sleep schedule. Since Senator was not fully awake, I clicked on the weather report to see if the day intended to cooperate with our plans to hike Diamond Head State Monument. We had originally planned to do it on Friday, but that was before the afternoon was wasted renting car #3.

As I was daydreaming about our itinerary and route, the television caught my eye. When we had been on the Big Island, other guests at the bed and breakfast had mentioned a hurricane that was supposed to be coming in during the middle of the next week, perhaps on Wednesday. We had not paid much attention since we would be leaving Monday evening. Thus, it was ignored and forgotten. Now the forecasters revealed that the hurricane would arrive on Honolulu earlier than expected. *Like how much earlier?* I wondered.

I watched intently as the animated arcs splashed over the map of the islands on the screen. Senator sat up and put his glasses on. "So basically it will be here within an hour of when our flight is supposed to leave?" he asked, not overly-concerned and not unconcerned. I stared at the screen and interpreted the expected landfall times, which were plastered at regular intervals on each island.

"Well, as far as I can tell... yes." It appeared our record for disasters occurring around our vacations was soundly intact. *Well this was certainly a conversation starter*

---

for your best interest. (Senator and Wendy V give it two resounding thumbs up.)

for our day. Illinois tornadoes we knew; tropical hurricanes were another matter.

For the next hour all focus was on strategic planning. When it became clear that we absolutely were not going to fly out at the scheduled time, Senator wisely decided to be proactive and book a flight that would get us out earlier- either Monday morning or Sunday night. Monday morning would not be so bad, but I hated the thought of cutting the already-abbreviated vacation short another day. For all of our exploring, we had not even been in the ocean yet.

I listened in as Senator spoke with an airline agent. "Okay, Monday morning? 7:30am? Yeah, that's good..." I could live with this, but I dreaded the thought of separate seats for so many hours. "Yes, two seats together," he continued. *Ah, very good. This could work well...* "What?! You're telling me that, even though the airline knows that a hurricane is coming and it will be canceling flights, it will not waive the change fee? Then never mind. Thank you." He hung up.

In other words, by trying to prevent further problems and sparing the airline two more people to deal with when the poi hit the fan, they would prefer to ignore the inevitable and maintain shyster policy. Cutting our vacation short would *cost* us $450. Even Senator, who can spend money in moments of desperation far easier than I can, flatly refused. That was settled, but nothing else was. There were still questions of possibly being stranded, with or without a vehicle, depending on rental guidelines. We also wondered if we would need to find lodging for an extra night. How and where would that take place? It was frustrating not knowing, but there was nothing we could do until our flight was officially canceled, so we slathered on our sunscreen and left for the southern coast of Oahu.

The drive was beautiful, giving little hint of the impending atmospheric doom. Endless sapphire waves pounded beaches-- some made of sand, others made of black lava boulders. In one cove the tidal rush was particularly violent, shooting water up through a blow hole with each incoming smack. A few surfers dotted the coastline, anxious for the larger waves that precede a hurricane. Most people were just out enjoying a warm, sunny Sunday morning in Hawai'i, though.

Eventually we reached Diamond Head. The well known landmark is an extinct crater, made famous mostly because of its distinct brown bowl that accidentally ends up in the background of most pictures of Waikiki Beach. As such, it is a tourist attraction, but we hoped that most people would not bother to actually hike its trail. Not so. A giant line of traffic snaked its way up the crater. Upon reaching the entrance, a small sign informed us that the insufficient parking lot was full.

Back down the crater we drove, noting at some point that we had passed the point of reasonably being able to walk to the top. In seeing Diamond Head from that perspective, however, I cannot say we were heartbroken. Looking out, we realized that we would have been hiking on an internal circular trail. Ergo, until we reached the rim, our view would basically be the other side of the big, brown bowl. So much for Diamond Head.

The southern coast of Oahu is surprisingly rugged. I guess I find it surprising because it seems like the throngs of tourists should have somehow worn away its rocky crags, inlets, and outlets. I was happy to see that its relatively close proximity to Honolulu has not spoiled it so far. The other unique aspect about this part of the island is its position. Situated where the windward and leeward coasts collide, it ranges from desert to tropics within less distance than my daily commute.

We stopped along the coast to watch the surf and examine the tidal pools. More black crabs like the ones we saw on the Big Island scuttled among inky black rock and occasionally grabbed for trapped fish. Looking southeast, it was hard to imagine that a hurricane would be on the horizon the next day. There was no indication of this, so we continued to balance and hop our way around the beach for another half hour before realizing how dehydrated we had become. Sun and wind were taking their toll.

The drive to buy a few bottles of water was longer than expected. Why we were not traveling with a case of it I do not know, but the more we thought about it, the thirstier we became. Always the ocean was in the backdrop. *Water, water, everywhere, nor any drop to drink.**

Finally, after backtracking many scenic miles, we found a gas station in a small but busy town. Birthday parties, church picnics, and community fairs all took place simultaneously along various stretches of beach. As elsewhere in Hawai'i, driving the main highway gave us a

---

*   from "The Rime of the Ancient Mariner" by Samuel Taylor Coleridge

front row seat to all of it, including the not-so-pretty parts.*

We left the gas station and drove back to a trailhead we had spotted earlier. It climbed back into a steep hill and appeared to lead to a lighthouse about halfway up the cliffs. From there, the views would be magnificent. I was also eager to see a remote Pacific lighthouse.

We parked the car in the almost-full lot, grabbed our water (dummies), and began the mile path upward. It was paved, but it was very steep. Within moments, our heart rates were up. Soon we could barely talk to each other. Focused, we spiraled on.

Our "mile" was really 1.4 miles. Though the ocean comprised three-quarters of our view, there was no denying we had entered a desert. A few scrubby trees gave way to shorter brush and arid-climate plants. At one point a plaque kindly informed us that we were occupying an excellent perch for whale watching, provided it was winter. Ironically, it was now summer, which meant that the whales were along the coast of northern California, where we had also missed them by visiting there in spring. Clearly the world's largest mammals were avoiding us.

We had something stranger to watch than whales, however. Hovering in the sky were four brave souls who were hang gliding. Strapped into contraptions resembling parachutes, they rode the breezes, sometimes struggling to maintain control. They were mesmerizing to watch, but I had to turn my eyes away every time it looked like they would either hurl into the cliffs or plummet to the ground

---

* We later learned that many of the primitive beach campsites were crude shelters used by the homeless.

several hundred feet below. Fortunately for me, (and more fortunately for them,) I witnessed no such catastrophe.

In another fifteen minutes we reached the top. We looked around, noting the glaring absence of any lighthouse. "Oh, there it is," I said, pointing downward. We had taken a longer trail that sent us further out and higher above it. We now had an even more extensive view. "Well, I guess that works, too..." Senator was satisfied, and we now had an entirely downhill hike to anticipate.

By the time we reached the bottom and marched the extra half-mile to the car, we were hot, sweaty, and tired. The Burning Black Box (also known as rental car #3), had saved all of the afternoon's most intense heat for us. Inside, we sucked down another bottle of water between us. No more hikes during this vacation. "Want to go in the water?" suggested Senator. *Hhmmm, go into the ocean while visiting Hawai'i? What a novel idea!*

An hour later we were wearing more sunscreen and less clothing. We walked along the shore for awhile, nothing how clean the beach was. We definitely weren't in Chicago anymore, Toto. Before long we convinced ourselves to go wading, but I was leery about going out too far. This actually backfired. Whereas Senator was riding the waves and bouncing along merrily in water up to his neck, I was being pelted and slapped down by each gentle sweep because I was only in up to my thighs. I corrected it, and we goofed off for about an hour. It was just long enough to have fun and cross "swimming in ocean" off of our list.

Back at our base we checked the progress of

Hurricane Flossie. It had slowed down somewhat, but it was still on track to hit each major island in succession. We decided to gas up the Burning Black Box, so at least we would not have to worry about that later. Otherwise, there was nothing else to do but eat some dinner and try to relax for the night.

In hurricane proactive move #2, Senator called the owner of the rental apartment, who lived on the property. Perhaps he could offer some useful insight. In the words of Will, (who incidentally was a native Iowan,) "Nah, don't worry about it. They're just excited because it's the first one in about twenty years."[*] As it turns out, meteorologists regularly study the phenomenon of why Hawai'i is rarely bothered by hurricanes, unlike other islands in warm climates.

We were not worried about safety as much as how we would successfully coordinate our escape from paradise. It was time to leave. We had accomplished everything we had come to Hawai'i to experience, and we were ready to go. The logistics of the next twenty-four hours would be tricky, though. Naturally our airline was not bothering to update our flight status. 1.3 million Hawai'ians knew that a hurricane was on the way, but this minor fact had managed to slip by United unnoticed. (This was a particularly impressive piece of mismanagement when one considers that their runways are so close to the Pacific Ocean that they are often splashed.) Since no more decisions could be made at that time, we went to bed.

*   *   *

---

[*] This fact should surprise no reader of this series.

Monday morning, our last day in Hawai'i, I had finally adjusted to the time zone change. That figured. I would have easily continued to sleep on if Senator was not awake and alert, faithfully taking the reins of hurricane patrol. The reporter of the t.v. informed us that Flossie had been downgraded to a tropical storm (good), but it/she was still scheduled to nail Honolulu with strong winds and waves exactly when we were supposed to be taking off (not good). At this point, our plans finally began to fall into place.

Step #1: We called United yet again, and this time they had officially canceled our flight. *Well thank you for that news flash. Too bad you didn't let us reschedule yesterday.*

Step #2: Senator beat the crowds of displaced tourists and immediately got on the phone with a live airline agent. His efficiency paid off, and he booked us a nonstop flight from Honolulu to Chicago the next morning, twelve hours after our originally scheduled flight. He was even able to get us two seats together. In an odd coincidence, out of hundreds of seats on the plane, they were the exact same two seats we had originally reserved. It may sound silly, but we were both relieved to know we had a ticket back to the mainland.

Step #3: Since we would not be leaving until early Tuesday morning, we needed somewhere to sleep on Monday night. Thus, the first question: do we stay put and try to add another night at the apartment we were currently occupying or go back to Honolulu? Staying in Kailua would be a nicer experience, and easier since we would not have to pack and relocate again. On the other hand, as much as we despised Waikiki, it was much closer to the airport, which could be useful if roads were flooded or transportation became an issue. Back to Honolulu it was, just to be on the safe side.

I pulled out my travel notes and called the only hotel number in Honolulu that I knew. It was where we had stayed the first night, so at least we would know how to find it... provided they were not already booked solid by other travelers in our predicament. As I waited for someone to answer, I tried to formulate a list of alternate hotels, but my mind only returned to the many horror stories I had read in internet reviews. Palm trees blowing sideways was one thing; roaches marching around our luggage was quite another. Of course there were more upscale places, but at 400 bucks a night, the roaches were looking like potential roommates. Miraculously, the girl on the other end soon answered and offered me a choice of the only three rooms they had left, so I rattled off my credit card number to reserve the least expensive one.

So far, so good. We had a plane, a bed, and even a spare clean outfit or two. This hurricane thing was working out alright after all. We looked out the window at the shower that had started to splatter the ground. Nothing dramatic appeared yet, but who knew what we would witness before the end of the day? In the meantime, we still had to contend with the trickiest decision.

Step #4: Do we attempt to extend our rental on car #3 until the early Tuesday morning when our flight would leave, or do we dump it off late Monday afternoon as planned, and rely on other transportation to get us to the airport? We thoroughly examined our options over a mediocre breakfast in the world's slowest diner. Senator sipped his Kona coffee, (which by now had worn out its appeal and revealed itself to be only about #6 on our Top Coffees of All Time list). I took a deep breath and organized my thoughts, slightly distracted by the overly meaty dish the people at the next booth were eating. It was raining harder now.

"If we keep the car until tomorrow morning, we know we have a way to get to the airport. We also know we have our own wheels if they announce a mass evacuation, which could be more useful than hoping the aloha spirit would move a local to pick up two drenched hitchhikers and their luggage," I ventured.

"True, but we could also end up driving on very busy highways, that may be rerouting us onto detours, while navigating through 6-10 inches of rain. And that's if they even let us keep the car longer," Senator countered.

"Good point-- I don't want you driving us while under that kind of stress," I agreed. (After all, somewhere amid this mess, we were supposed to be enjoying our last day in Hawai'i.) "Plus, what if we go to return the car and no one's there to receive it because it's too early in the morning, or because they are under water? We would either have to abandon the car or miss our flight, both of which would probably result in me getting arrested.[*] We agreed to return the car that afternoon, which led to our craziest transportation plan to date.

After breakfast we dodged through the rain and into

---

[*]   because at that point I would likely hurt someone

the Burning Black Box, which had morphed into simply the Humid Box. Traffic was already picking up as people left work early to beat Flossie home, but we reached Honolulu safely and easily returned the car. The rental agency did not offer shuttles to the Waikiki hotels, but they did run a circuit to the airport. Happy to not be responsible for any more driving, we boarded the shuttle for Honolulu International. "Which airline?" asked the driver.

"Um, United," I answered, probably sounding like a kid trying to cover a lie badly. It did not really matter where we were dropped off, but we were the most familiar with that terminal. The scheme we had devised required backtracking to the airport to take one of their complimentary shuttles to our hotel. As it turned out, navigating one's way from "Departures" to "Arrivals" was easier said than done. Eventually though, we found ourselves sweating on the curbside, scoping the various shuttle buses for the one which we had called.

It did not come. Twenty minutes later, every shuttle for every hotel and every car rental company had passed by, yet ours was nowhere in sight. It was hot, and the only shady patch had to be shared with an active smoker. Our patience was running out, and we were one step away from getting on each other's nerves, which was not a place we wanted to be... on our last afternoon in paradise... as a hurricane sped toward us.

"When you called, you didn't give any credit card number, right?" I asked Senator, probably sharper than I meant to.

"No," he confirmed, working slightly less diligently

95

to conceal his growing annoyance. Senator glanced at me sideways, halfway wondering what I was cooking up, and halfway not wanting to know.

When the next Waikiki-bound shuttle pulled to the curb, I approached the driver, trying to appear cute, dumb, needy, and any other stereotype that would have set women's lib back fifty years. "Hi! Can you take us to the Ilima Hotel?" I made very direct eye contact. He scanned his reservation list, which, of course, did not contain our names. Meanwhile it had started to mist, and quickly changed to a sprinkle. This was not helping the mood, so I concentrated my mental powers on sending a distinct just-get-us-to-a-dry-room-and-I-will-make-it-worth-your-while message.

"Yeah, okay, yeah," he agreed. It had begun to rain harder. We wheeled our luggage to the rear door and let the driver take over as we settled into our seats. Another phase was complete, and just in time.

The pouring rain reduced visibility significantly. Had we still been driving, I might have gotten us lost, or Senator might have gotten into an accident. This way was much better, if less adventurous. (Plus, we liked each other again.)

I leaned against Senator and we slouched together as mentally exhausted spectators. I could not see much out the window, but I did happen to catch a glimpse of the very belated shuttle that was originally supposed to rescue us as it pulled up to the curb. *Aloha, suckers!* For all we know, they may still be there waiting...

There was also the entertainment factor associated

with taking the shuttle. In the boarding process we were joined by several other people, including the Egocentric Couple. These presumably Midwestern middle-agers proudly illustrated every facet for which tourists are loathed by locals, including-- though not admittedly-- Hawai'ians. In their loud floral shirts and straw hats, they sprawled out across the entire row of seats. Once situated awkwardly, they proceeded to grandly and obliviously discuss their upcoming week with everyone on board, most of whom would have banded together to strangle them had we not wanted to avoid any further stress on our driver.[*]

As our long-suffering chauffeur navigated traffic jams and torrential rain in his mission to safely deliver us to five different Waikiki[†] hotels, the couple's interrogation of him began. "Where does that trolley go?" *Probably anywhere that you are not.* "What's the best way to do Pearl Harbor?" *From underneath.* "When is the market open?" *The day you leave.* Interspersed, naturally, were the couples' narrations of lunch plans. "Oooohh, a Subway..." "Cheesecake Factory! I know where I'm having lunch!" Senator's theory was that they booked a flight to Honolulu and made absolutely no plans beyond that. If only someone had written a guidebook, or published a travel brochure, or drawn a map, or created a website for folks visiting Hawai'i. Nope, these clowns were determined to turn the one individual who held our lives in his steering wheel into their personal Tour Guide for Dummies.

---

[*] Any jury would have deemed it justifiable homicide.
[†] a Hawai'ian word which I have come to believe means 'armpit of the islands' in English

Our stop was the last one. I'll give you one guess as to whose stop was second-to-last. At least we had a quiet, clean room. It also had a great view of the rain. And, thank goodness, it received the Scenic Hawai'i channel.

At some point we decided that we needed a last meal before the tropical storm rendered us alone, desperate, and hungry. Like a bad rerun, we set out on the same few blocks that we had traversed almost a week ago. This time we were in a downpour. As expected, nothing had changed; food was bad and objects in shops were hopelessly tacky. In fact, prior to that walk, I had taken some comfort in the fact that I had not seen any "I got lei'd in Hawaii" shirts, but I could no longer claim even that shred of dignity for Waikiki. Likewise, if one wanted to impress her friends with her tanned, toned, voluptuous body, she could certainly do so by plunking down $28.00 for the beach body tee shirt. (Surely no one would ever know that it was merely a stamped picture.)

As we nibbled a horrible vegan version of something erroneously claiming to be a burrito, a cute little lizard sat on a pipe and watched us in the intense humidity. We were outside, in a cramped, depressing, three-sided white cinder block box that served as 'patio' seating. I think the lizard pitied us, and rightly so. Being trapped in paradise really kind of sucked.

Back in the room we lamely alternated between the Weather Channel and Scenic Hawai'i. Every time we stepped out onto our balcony we were disappointed by the lack of action. The weather rotated between drizzle and hard rain, but we were not treated to any of the dramatic waves that Midwesterners are led to believe accompany major tropical storms. The most interesting aspect of our view was the tourists hop-stepping across giant puddles while bumping into each other's umbrellas.

We stepped back inside and Senator went to take a shower. I automatically clicked back to the Weather Channel again. At least it had started to thunder a little. Occasionally it was accented by a lightning flash. "Hey, I've got a flashlight ready in case the hotel loses power," I yelled into the bathroom, not bothering to get up.

The man on the television, whose paycheck was directly related to the amount of alarm he interjected, desperately warned me to "stay away from windows and seek shelter". We were sure trying, but our shelter was thousands of miles away.

To emphasize the threat, he cut to the anchorman, who introduced a home video clip some brave viewer had sent in. The footage captured what we would call an average spring storm. The guys filming it were far more impressed. "Did you see *that*?!" one hollered. "It was incredible-- lightning everywhere!" This was not only sucky; it was downright boring.*

As we settled in to get a few hours of sleep, we kept telling ourselves that we would be home in less than twenty-four hours. Sooner or later we hoped to believe it. In the meantime we still felt trapped, without even a

---

* We were later informed that Hawai'i only sees lightning about ten days out of the year. That includes the entire island chain, so the odds of witnessing it on a single island are even smaller. That could explain why no one ever bothers to evacuate the water when it starts to rain.

captain, a professor, or a millionaire couple to help us. Thus, we fell asleep to the soothing sounds of Hurricane Flossie.

*   *   *

Before dawn we checked out of the hotel. We were bleary-eyed and haggard-looking, ironically highlighted by the cheap shell leis the desk clerk had bestowed upon us. Amid my mental fog, I thought of the "lei'd" tee shirt, and I wanted to go home more than ever. A pre-arranged car was waiting for us, and we tipped the driver generously for his role in abetting our escape. Before long we were deposited at the airport and situated on our flight.

Our journey home on flight #4 felt faster than it was, despite the annoying, chatty, bratty freshmen girls behind us. From their conversations, we judged them to be trust fund babies. Our belief in this assumption was strengthened when the flight attendant announced that one of the girls had a peanut allergy and asked that no one aboard eat any nuts. Given the junk the girl was consuming, it seemed like more of an attention issue than a looming medical crisis. We respected the dietary request, but by the end of the flight I was tempted to open a bag of Planters on her.

We landed and somehow managed to locate our luggage, despite no mention of which baggage carousel corresponded with our flight. We also managed to find our way to the monorail, despite signs that literally sent us in a circle. Finally, we managed to merge onto I-294, despite no exit signs showing the way to the highway. (God help foreigners who have to decipher O'Hare.)

It was 11:00pm in our native time zone. Our pizza binge coincided perfectly with Hawai'ian dinner time. We were home, probably for our longest 'dry' stretch, due to the no-longer-existent travel fund. For my part, I placed a moratorium on any further trip planning. Of course, planning does not include dreaming...

Chapter 3
Just Bluffin':
Early July 2014

By the end of the summer of 2013 we had visited fifty out of fifty united-- and sometimes separated by vast expanses-- states. Now what? That meant no urgent travel plans and no viable excuse to make them. The combination saw us shoving the luggage into the back of the closet for almost a year.

Not that I had much time to bemoan my plight, though. The first semester of the school year cruised by, gaining even more momentum after the holidays. As had been the pattern for the previous year, Senator's recording work continued to increase, bringing us more adventures in Chicago and Milwaukee. Though he had intended to look for additional work in March, we were blessed to discover there was no need for another job just yet.*

---

* At one point Senator got a hot tip on a job opening at our little town's library, located just two blocks from our home. Reasoning that bookstore experience and the potential of a one-minute commute could not be ignored, he decided to apply. Dressed up,

In a blink, summer school was starting, and in another blink it was wrapping up. Each day I would spend intermittent moments daydreaming about hitting the road again. By now it was tradition to spend a few days in Door County, Wisconsin, with our friends, and we were eagerly planning time to bike ride, cool off, enjoy the lake views, and indulge in much laughter and visiting. I even had about ten days off in between to take my time packing and catch up a bit at home.

Senator, on the other hand, decided to use one of our mornings off together to break his toe. Actually, though we have considered various options as to how to enhance the tale, the simple truth is that he walked downstairs barefoot, took a corner too fast or the wrong way, and plunged a chunk of his foot into the corner of an amplifier. Ow. Oh man, ow. Somehow we doubted that it was pure coincidence that it had been the same amp he had launched into a gravel parking lot after it had seemingly cut out on him while playing a live show.† As he elevated and iced under my strict direction, we decided that some armchair medical research was in order. Scanning various websites

---

with clean copy of resume in hand, he kissed me and walked out the door. I smiled as I finished my workout routine, saying a prayer that it would go in whatever way would be best for us. Seven minutes later he was back. The none-too-friendly librarian had curtly informed him that they "were not accepting applications at this time". He thought it better not to point out to her that that was, in fact, illegal. So be it. We were happy for a definitive sign.

† Later it appeared that the amp worked perfectly, so it was once again welcomed into the good graces of the basement studio, not without its bitter grudge, however.

we determined that it was either: 1.)broken or 2.)dislocated. If broken, too bad for you. Deal with it. If dislocated, it must be relocated-- correctly.

Like all well-informed citizens, I read just enough to scare myself. I had visions of an incorrectly set toe stifling Senator for life. Maybe he would be in pain far too long. Maybe his shoes would not fit anymore. Maybe he would never be able to hike! That did it. To be on the safe side, we agreed to take him to the express care clinic the next morning.

Several x-rays later, the verdict was that Senator had broken his toe. (See option #1.) I suggested we skip the planned Door County trip. He was determined to go. I suggested we make no attempt to bike ride. He claimed that riding was easier than walking. I strongly suggested that I drive. He strongly challenged himself to drive-- stick shift no less.

Senator continued to hobble and maneuver his way throughout various activities he wanted to accomplish. Sunday morning, exactly a week after the amp had bitten him, he strapped the bikes to the back of his car and carefully slid into the driver's seat. I had my doubts, but we were on our way. I hope if a heavy piece of equipment ever injures me I can maintain his positive attitude and sense of humor...

The drive progressed without incident, and we exited to a small Wisconsin town for gas. Guess who insisted on pumping? Senator finished filling the tank and walked (sort of) inside for a pit stop and a coffee. He then settled back into the car and situated himself to drive for a while longer.

As the coffee cooled to an almost-drinkable temperature, I noted how good it smelled. Yes, the car smelled very good indeed. Then I realized why. "Oh, shoot!" The cup had tipped back over the zarf* and was silently raining brewed caffeine down one side of the hump on the back floor. It reminded me of the volcano lava we never got to see.

Once again we stopped, each wondering how this could have happened. Upon further examination, the main victims were a bag (no big deal), the floor mat (probably going to be a problem), and the book-style cd holder (definitely not good). Senator sighed in annoyance once or twice. As I mopped up the Guatamalan lake with a mass of restroom paper towels, the only consolation I could offer was, "Well, at least you drink it black... Cream and sugar could have made a *real* mess..." At the moment, my Essential Other was not appreciating the positive spin on the event at hand, but we were soon on our way again, ultimately undeterred.

Amid damp drizzle outside and the moist aroma of roasted beans inside, we arrived in Fish Creek, glad to see Bill and Marge. Senator unpacked the car, and I arranged our things in our bedroom. Then Senator unpacked the cheese plate and we all arranged ourselves on the couches to watch the crazy antics of the squirrels outside the picture windows. There's a lot to be learned about creativity and determination from these creatures, though I know certain people close to me would disagree.

---

* Look it up. It's a real word. I promise.

Later that evening we walked the half block to go to a barn concert, located on the same property as the farmhouse in which we were staying. For the second year in a row, we were seeing folk singer Karen Mal perform in her breezy, homey, often poignant style. As we purchased our tickets, the property owner apologized several times for the noise from the concert the night before. Our friends had not been bothered by it, and we had not even been there then, all of which we mentioned to the owner. Oblivious to our explanations, he apologized some more. They say Wisconsinites are more polite than Illinoisans. I can believe it. We shrugged and found our seats.

We settled among the mostly older crowd, but I could not help noticing one Mom who had a younger kid with her. Naturally, the kid was bored out of his mind. He continued to scroll through his iPhone, his face illuminated an unearthly digital blue. Hey Mom, here's a thought: maybe ten-year olds aren't into folk music that hearkens back to thirty years before they were born. Maybe Junior isn't quite ready for full immersion into the acoustic singer/songwriter experience. They were not as disruptive as they could have been, I suppose, but no one missed them when they gave up and left at the break.

Back at the house it was time to initiate the movie/couch portion of the trip. The four of us found our adopted spots, and Senator presented our hosts with a 140-episode dvd series of *Robin Hood**. For the unacquainted, that's a lot of sheriff-battling and gold-redistributing. The dvd player must have been overwhelmed by the sheer

---

* late 1950s British version, starring Richard Green

grandeur of it, however, because it promptly died. That was alright; it was nothing a little berry cheesecake and good conversation couldn't fix.

*   *   *

It continued to drizzle throughout the night Sunday, and Monday was the only day with a clear forecast, so it was designated cruise day. Before the others got too far into their morning routine, I slipped out for a short bike ride down the familiar country roads. The breeze was cool and the traffic light, making me wish I could spend an extra hour or two riding. Senator was still nursing a broken toe, and biking did not sound as appealing as elevating his foot while drinking coffee and watching the morning feeding frenzy of the birds. As I pedaled back, I noticed the maple sugar grove that we had visited the year before. We would have to make a point of stocking up on the northern nectar.

On this particular day, Bill and Marge had generously booked a boat tour for the four of us. This was no sun-yourself-and-nap-in-the-breeze deal, mind you. We were on a serious mission. The aptly-named Lighthouse Cruise would take us past an operating lighthouse or two on Lake Michigan, but more importantly, it would bring us up close and personal with several non-operating lighthouses, which are infinitely more intriguing to people with too much imagination.

Prior to going to the port, we had to stop at Koepsel's. You will no doubt remember that the Koepsels are the unknowing patron saints of all of our Door County picnics. Their farm store is a fantastic island of all things rural, edible, and jarred. For this day's purposes, we selected pickled garlic, pickled pickles, and pecan crunch (not pickled, since it never lasts long enough to need preserving).

We took our feast to a bench at the end of the port's parking lot. Roaring up from the Green Bay side of the peninsula was a wonderful breeze that kept our hair out of our pickles. Despite the wind, we also attempted to record a podcast episode, easily passing the thirty minutes until our vessel launched. When we finished, we packed our gear, sauntered down the small hill, and met Jim and Judy.

Jim was our captain, and he was happy to share his expertise, based on many years of navigating Death's Door. Judy was his wife, and she was happy to share her expertise, which included useful tidbits such as how much the very expensive bluff-top estates were worth, and that we should use the bathroom before climbing aboard. She opened the storage area under the bow and indicated the portable camp toilet that would be some poor soul's only option if he/she did not heed Judy's words. Once fourteen empty-bladdered passengers had boarded, we left the shoreline for the open water.

As we clipped along, we could see several caves in the sides of the bluffs. Thick trees lined the top rim, broken only by vacation properties of the rich and unknown. We then pulled into a small inlet that led us to the edge of Plum Island. This uninhabited isle held the original lighthouse for the region in 1848. A decade later the light was moved, but Plum Island continued to serve in the Twentieth Century as a U.S. life saving service station as well as a U.S. Coast Guard station. Currently, the only people who get to see it are the fun-sounding F.O.P.P.I. (Friends of Plum and Pilot Islands) members, and they pay $100 for the membership and its privileges.

Backing away from Plum Island, we set our sights on the highlight of the two-hour tour-- Pilot Island. We bounced our way through a few wakes from other boats, but it soon seemed like our little clipper was very alone... except for the birds. Pilot Island had grabbed our attention for as long as we had known about it. During our first visit to see our friends, in 2008, we took the ferry from the mainland to Washington Island. Midway during the ride, Marge pointed out an ominous-looking island to the east, completely dilapidated and overrun with flocks of gulls and cormorants. Of course we have wanted to see it up-close ever since then, and we finally had our chance.

As we approached the foreboding island, the waves of bird screams grew louder. For about a century, from the mid-1800s to the mid-1900s, the 3½-acre Pilot Island was a functioning lighthouse. Functioning did not always mean pleasant, however. Isolation was severe, and the life of a keeper and his family was difficult.[*]

When the last tenders left in 1962, the birds moved in, and made more birds, and made a general mess of the island. In particular, the feces of cormorants contained something toxic to the habitat, effectively killing all of the vegetation on the island. The bare tree limbs only serve to enhance the creepy background. Not often treated to visitors, hundreds of avian eyes stared down our boat and

---

* For detailed stories on the lives of Pilot Island Lighthouse tenders, visit: www.lighthousefriends.com.

its passengers. We spent some time admiring the 3-D Hitchcockian scene before our boat pulled away to head back.

After our cruise tour ended, we left for the second adventure of the day. We were still trying to wring every minute out of the only sunny day of our trip, so we drove toward Door Bluff Headlands County Park. After years of coming up to Door County, our friends had pretty much explored every nook and cranny of the mainland. Somehow, though, Door Bluff has escaped Marge's careful planning radar. Coincidentally, I had spied it on the internet a few weeks prior and also wanted to check it out. From my research, it looked easy enough to find, yet quiet enough to be a respite from the tourists. Even better, the access road to the park was just around the corner from Gill's Rock, where our boat tour was docked.

Or it should have been. The close-up map showed one main road. We saw one main road. In fact, we were on it. It followed the same general direction that the representative line on the map did. Eight eyeballs could not spy anything resembling a park entrance, so we backtracked to a side road that had split off a few miles back. It went against my gut feeling, but we did not have a better option, so we tried it.

When it became clear that the side road was even further from anything that could physically amount to a bluff than the main road was, we started over. Back to Gill's Rock we drove. Thankfully, it had not moved since we were last there. Marge took one for the team and ducked into a gift shop to ask for directions. Sure enough, we had been on the correct road the first time, but we had not gone far enough. *But it was only about two inches on the map...*

We drove the main road again, through considerably wealthy neighborhoods. "Maybe the people who live here want to keep the park obscured from people like us," suggested Bill. Very possible. I had visions of imported British butlers and suspicious gardeners all giving us the evil eye. At least we were climbing higher, which is decidedly more assuring when scouting out a bluff. Once in a while we could see the bay peak out between the dense trees, which we also took as a good sign.

Finally we reached the top, which dead-ended at... nothing. I do not remember if there was a sign or not, but there sure wasn't much else. There was no view of the water, no picnic area, nowhere to park, and no point-- geographically or otherwise. There was only a tiny turnaround that looped near an outhouse. One truck with a trailer appeared to be waiting, although I can't imagine for what. Maybe someone in their party was taking advantage of the bathroom, if it was even unlocked. Booo.

We ruled that Door Bluff Headlands County Park was actually located somewhere else, where no tourists were welcome. The faux park was merely a ruse to scare us back to the main highway. Still determined to have a picnic somewhere near water and decent scenery, we drove back down the road and found another turnoff. This time, we found a gravel parking lot, complete with unlocked port-a-potty. Across from the lot was a very small beach with several picnic-worthy boulders. The four of us carried our odd assortment of jarred foods and crossed the road.

We had arrived at the "Silent Sports" boat ramp, according to the sign. Apparently it was a place to launch one's kayak, canoe, paddle boat, or library. The only people in the area were a single woman in a bikini and a man unloading his kayak from his SUV. Bikini Woman was walking along the beach and smoking (silently). SUV man, on the other hand, kept his motor running for a full twenty minutes while he pondered the finer points of 1.)whether he actually wanted to kayak, 2.)how he could place the kayak in the water if the answer to #1 was "yes", 3.)where in the world he was, and 4.)how he, in fact, arrived there.

As the lost kayaker mulled things over, Bill, Marge, Senator, and I claimed our rock-seats and opened up our goodies. Once again we brought out the small, portable recorder that documented our stories and general silliness. Most of the first half-hour episode we recorded was set to the gentle hum of a motor running. Eventually, though, the would-be kayaker decided to take his talents elsewhere. Once he was gone, there was only the sound of light waves splashing the sand and rocks. Ah, picnic.

We wrapped up our afternoon and began the drive back to the house. As a group, our evenings in Door County could hardly be a commercial for the region's night life. Generally they center around movies, games, and all that is wonderful about a night in. To remedy the lack of movie-viewing ability, we made a quick stop to buy a new dvd player.

Back at the house, it was on to more squirrel monitoring and general relaxation. I'm always amazed at how fast I can finish a book without a pesky job to get in the way. We napped, read, drew, and visited until it was time to venture back out. Yes, I realize this contradicts the previous paragraph, but we were not on our way to some bar, club, or entertainment venue. Instead, we needed the proper background to listen to a radio show.

We first stopped for dinner, opting to sit outside and watch the sun set. As we sat down, a few drops of rain began. Just as we got our table's umbrella opened, the rain stopped, naturally. Though it was no longer raining, some dark, low-hanging clouds were moving in swiftly, preparing for a good drenching the next day. Good-- it all added to the ambiance we were trying to create.

We finished our dinner and drove across the street to the marina at Bailey's Harbor. Bill parked the car, and we all got comfortable. It was an hour or so past sunset, and the wide clearing gave a sweeping view of the blue-black sky and a distant lighthouse. Occasional showers dotted the windows. Now we were ready to listen to *Three Skeleton Key*. I won't retell the story, but if you ever find yourself in a dark harbor, and you spy a derelict ship in the distance, take great caution, particularly if the brown ship seems to be "undulating"...

After we had sufficiently recovered from *Three Skeleton Key*, it was time to go back to the house and lighten the mood. This was first achieved by finding suitable sweets. Then it was enhanced by watching a few episodes of Robin Hood putting the Sheriff of Nottingham in his place, (and Maid Marion putting Robin Hood in *his* place). Once the merry band was again situated in Sherwood

Forest, we turned in for the night.

*   *   *

Tuesday morning the clouds were already gathering, but I wanted to take another short bike ride anyway. If I got wet, I got wet. I explained what I was doing to Senator, who wasn't fully awake yet. He nodded, and mumbled that I take a phone and not be gone too long. I could tell that he probably would not be able to join me on any bike rides while in Door County, despite his admirable determination.

I made the same run as the previous morning. Two turns down to a stop sign, then backtracking past the fields. I was unpleasantly startled when I realized-- perhaps thankfully too late-- that I had passed very closely to a black and yellow snake. In retrospect, I think it was actually dead, but I was creeped out nonetheless. My mood improved significantly just before returning to the house, though. The farm that produced its own maple syrup had turned its sign to "OPEN".

I hopped off my bike at the house, greeting a more awake Senator. I told him about the likely-dead snake and how shaken up I was. More importantly, I told him that real maple syrup was available just yards from where we stood. I put away my bike as he informed our friends that we would be back in fifteen minutes.

This time we pledged to load up. Why not buy plenty? We were supporting a local farm, who was in turn providing us with excellent real maple syrup. Nothing we could get at home would compare to this.

We drove up the driveway and got out of the car.

No one seemed to be around, so we sort of milled around awkwardly. The sign still announced that they were open, so I wandered the perimeter of the vibrant perennial garden. Either someone would come out to sell us syrup, or we could claim to be dumb tourists who were so impressed with the flowers that we had to stop. Eventually we decided to go to the door and knock. At first there was no answer, but just as we were about to give up, an older woman came to the door. As she was about to direct us to the sugar shack out back, her husband intervened.

Along with many quarts of maple syrup, we got a history lesson. The man had made syrup from the sap of the property's trees for the past seventy years. *No wonder it was so delicious!* The farm had also been in his family for fifty years prior to that. It was hard to picture so much stability in today's mobile society. The farmer went on to sadly explain that he wasn't sure who would take over when he and his wife could no longer do it. *Hey Senator... well, no, I guess that wouldn't work...* We concluded our conversation and paid for the syrup, which was lined up atop the antique stove and sink. The maple syrup was already a great value. The additional portrait of a local legacy was priceless.

We again met Bill and Marge and told them about the farm down the road, presenting them with their own bottle of amber liquid history. We were all just about ready to head to the southern end of the peninsula to Sturgeon Bay. The rain showers would make a fitting backdrop to visit the Door County Maritime Museum. Before we left, Senator suggested I double check on the information regarding their tug boat tours. That sounded like a good idea, so I called.

"Hi, I was just wondering how your tug boat tours work."

"Well, we have a docked tug boat and there are guided tours every day. It doesn't go out." Good-- that was what I had understood from my reading, so I proceeded.

"Right. Do we need to make a reservation?"

"Well, you can, but we don't really do that. You can just come and they leave several times per day." Basically I *could* make a reservation except that I could *not* make a reservation. Either way, I would have no idea for what time.

"Do the tours leave on the hour?" It seemed like a reasonable question.

"Well, it depends when the first one starts for the day, but the last one leaves at 3:30."

"Okay, I see [lie]. We'll just come down." Sometimes it is just easier to go and find out firsthand.

The four of us hit the highway, and in about a half hour we were there. The sky was a dark gray, which made the museum's colorful nautical flags stand out. It was pouring, so we made a mad dash for the door. When I walked inside to the information desk to buy tickets, I met the person who had been on the other end of my useless phone inquiry.

In a very precise and unnaturally monotone voice she rattled off a rehearsed speech about tickets, exhibits, and height minimums for children who wanted to tour the tug boat. Partly to break the ice and partly to determine whether she really was a cyborg, I smiled and told her that I was the shortest one in our party. She responded in her strange unbroken manner. "Yes-I-know-what-you-mean-I-am-the-shortest-person-out-of-five-kids-so-here-are-your-tickets-and-meet-right-there-at-two-for-your-tour." Aha-- so we had a definite time of 2:00 at least. Success!

There was plenty of time before the tour, so we wandered the galleries. One focused on shipbuilding history, which is a marvel in and of itself. I can't even imaging coordinating everything that would have to happen in the engine room, let alone every other facet of the ship. Heck, even the hollow models had me dazzled.

Another exhibit featured a display about pirates. While it was decidedly kid-oriented, it was still impressive. Tidbits of information separated fact from fiction, all surrounded by a walk-through gallery. Most of the exhibit gave the feel of actually being on an old ship, but I couldn't shake the image of Disneyworld's Pirates of the Caribbean ride from my head. Not that that's a bad thing...

My favorite part of the main museum was the Lighthouse Gallery. Here light tenders' stories were told through diaries, interviews, and photographs. As you can imagine, chores were tough, hours were long, and conveniences and guests were few. The most memorable story was about one keeper who was given a 20-day leave to go find a wife. Reportedly, he was unsuccessful. I guess he must not have been a fast worker.

The four of us walked back downstairs to meet for the tug boat tour. Soon our guide met us and a few others. He cautioned that we would be in tight quarters, and some tricky stairs were involved. I took that as promising.

Our first stop was the cable room. At least, that is what I named it in my head. About eight of us crammed inside, forming a 'u' around a large spool. Our guide explained that it took about 2,000 feet of cable to keep the vessel that was being towed steady and at a safe distance behind the tug boat.

The next stop was the engine room. In a word, it could only be described as intricate. Multiple levels of catwalks wound their way around giant engine parts and thousands of rivets. Vintage gauges could be seen on every major component, pointing too far to the right when pressure, temperature, or some other factor was out of its proper range. Though immaculate and brightly lit, the factory-like room struck me as kind of depressing.

If, like me, the deckhands found the engine room depressing, I had bad news for them regarding their quarters. Ranking officers enjoyed cozy bunk cabins with windows looking out from a second- or third- story view. The lowest class of workers on the ship basically went into a dark hole for their rest and relaxation. I think I would have opted to sleep outside on the deck.

We moved on to the mess area, which was tailored for life off the land. Cupboards had rails to rein in dishes that might be riding some particularly bouncy waves. I also seem to remember that the seats were stationary. As elsewhere on the ship, space was at a premium. Everything had to justify any volume it was taking up, and efficiency was the law of the land, or sea, as the case may be. Every item served a purpose and belonged to a specific place.

Our final stop before heading outside onto the deck was the bridge room. Here is where the view was grandest, taking in a wide panorama of the water. Here is also where we secretly named our tour guide Sad Bob. While he had been informative and pleasant enough, he really did not seem to enjoy his job.

With apparent frustration he told us that he had been so busy that he had barely had time to make some copies that he needed to make. *Times are tough all over, Pal...* When someone in our group asked if there was any chance that the tug boat would ever sail again, he took a deep breath and responded in his melancholy way, "We've had a million dollar restoration, but that was just for cosmetic purposes. It's never going to run." Though I had already assumed the vessel was permanently docked, I did not expect him to add, "We don't even know how long she'll stay afloat..."

"Hopefully for the next ten minutes at least," I couldn't help but joking. I received a muffled chuckle or two, but only a blank stare from Sad Bob. He concluded his talk and dutifully reminded us to stop by the gift shop. I hope the rest of his day went better...

It was pouring out as we left the Door County Maritime Museum, and the many shades of Great Lakes gray were competing. Bill drove us back to the middle of the peninsula, mentioning that he wanted to attempt something he called a "rolling podcast" at some point. It sounded like something goofy enough for us to try, so we added it to the agenda. Since we were all hungry, we only stopped at the house for a few moments before going for some sandwiches and greasy tavern fries.

We took our time and savored the last of the comfort food. We may have also indulged in a cup of coffee, as the temperature had dropped significantly. I was not complaining, since I'd rather have a 40-degree July than a 90-degree July. "So when should we do this 'rolling podcast'?" I ventured.

"Well, I thought maybe when we left here we could start the recorder. I can meander around so the trip back takes thirty minutes, and we can just converse and record an episode as we go," Bill suggested. That sounded good, so we paid our bill and walked out to the car. Once everyone was situated, Senator hit the magic red button, and we were on.

For some reason, at several points in the four-way conversation, we brought up the subject of ice cream. I do not remember what we said about it, but Senator started joking about wanting some. Then we learned he was not joking; the boy had a serious craving. Finding ice cream suddenly became our ridiculous mission-- one which ignored the fact that we had needed the heat on in the car the entire time. The first place was closed, but the second choice was open for business. Anticipating the needs of crazy people like ourselves, they also had giant outdoor warming lamps going as we chattered our order through the window. Eventually we gave up trying to eat our treats outside and went inside with the only-halfway-crazy people.

Wrapping up the rolling podcast, we pulled into the driveway of the house. It was pajama pants and couch time. We had plenty of sugar in our system. All that was left to do was knock out a few more *Robin Hood* shows. Maybe we would stay awake through more than one of them.

*　　　　　*　　　　　*

Wednesday morning opened our last full day in Door County. I was feeling too lazy to ride my bicycle, so I opted for a walk instead. It also gave me a chance to check out some of the trees and wildflowers up close. Contrary to the weather report, the sky was partly sunny.*

When I got back to the house, Senator was busy getting ready inside, so I plopped myself on the picnic table bench to make a phone call. About a week and a half prior, my sister had had a baby boy. My parents were officially grandparents, and they had gone to visit the new little man out of state. I was anxious to hear their reactions. My mom's voice beamed over the phone. "Oh Wendy, I know you'll laugh at me for saying this, but he really is just sooo cute and snuggly. We just love him!"

She was right. I could not help but tease here a little bit. "Well it's your grandson. What else would you say? That the kid's ugly and annoying?" I laughed. Thankfully so did she. I was glad everyone was happy and healthy, especially since I wouldn't get to meet Judah for several more months.

We finished our conversation and I joined Senator, Bill, and Marge to start out on one more excursion. Door Bluff Headlands, you will recall, distinctly sucked. Ergo, Marge and I were determined to find an alternative bluff

---

* or perhaps partly cloudy; I have no idea what the difference is.

more suitable to our standards. We had each noticed--again separately, since we are on the same wavelength-- a place called Ellison Bluffs on the map. Not to be lured into a wild goose chase again, she contacted the local information center for the inside scoop.

This time we were assured that it would live up to our expectations. We were promised a picnic area, with a scenic overlook. This was more like it. What's that? A bonus? We were told there was also ample parking and even a bathroom, albeit pit-style. We agreed that there darned well better be. If not, we unanimously decided to name our informant Lyin' Alice*.

To her credit, Truthin' Alice steered us well. We claimed a promised picnic table for lunch (check), after parking the car (check) and visiting the little hikers' room (check). We were probably 100 feet up, and a walkway took us down a little further to an expansive view. For the slightly braver, a metal catwalk extended out over the bluff. We tried it, but only for a few moments.

The highlight of the experience was that we were perfectly situated to watch a storm roll in across the bay. Coming in from the west, we had a front row seat to various cloud formations and movements. We could almost predict the minute the rain would reach us. When it did finally hit, it was a gentle sprinkle that coincided nicely with our plans to move along.

One of the great rainy afternoon pastimes for people

---

* in reference to a park ranger who had once gave us an inaccurate picture of certain hiking conditions; Bill named him Lyin' Jimmy.

like me is to browse an old, dusty bookstore.* This particular established shop boasted 70,000 volumes. Unfortunately, it soon became clear that 69,842 of them were overpriced, ripe for the tourists. Case in point: I found a locally published book about lighthouse tales marked at more than twice what I had paid for it in a bookstore near my home. Oh well. The books were interesting, and the crotchety owner was amusing, although I don't think he was happy with our lack of purchasing.

Later that evening we went out again for Mexican food, to the place with the chairs in the bathroom.† We ingested a nice layer of warm food, savoring it, as the night was drizzly again. Yes, it was damp and chilly, which apparently puts my Essential Other in the mood for a cold dessert. Like the previous night, he had a taste for ice cream. I had to admit, it did sound good, so we stopped in our friends' favorite spot to get cones. Then we sat outside under a covered porch to eat them. Why not? Would we do this at home? Not likely, but here we were, alternating between licks and shivers.

To recover from our frozen indulgence, we joined Bill and Marge back inside their heated car. Originally we had planned to walk or sit along the marina, but soft, dry car seats were more appealing than cold, hard, wet benches. As we sat parked, we recorded another episode of Bill's

---

* Somewhere Senator just sneezed. While he is a fan of books and reading, he is turned off by old, used books. I see history; he sees mold. I feel romance; he feels allergic.

† See the chapter "Pickled Podcasting" in *How to Hitch a Ride With No Thumbs*

podcast. On one of the docked boat decks we saw a man endlessly mopping. It seemed a little pointless, but maybe I'm just lazy. Come to think of it, it's probably a good thing that I do not have a boat. Come to think of it further, that type of boat was probably bigger than my entire yard. Nope, definitely crossing yacht off of my list.

The night concluded with a few hot rounds of Yahtzee. If you are not familiar with the popular dice game, its operation blends chance and strategy, somewhat like poker. It is fairly simple to learn, and fairly easy to get sucked into. While it is fun to win against one's opponents, a hardcore player really strives to beat his own record. When he rolls an elusive "Yahtzee", generally anyone playing will be excited for him. If he Yahtzees* a second, or even a third time, they will gasp in awe while he dares to hope that this could be the game where he achieves a new gaming pinnacle within his Yahtzee career. Rolling any additional Yahtzees beyond that, however, will lead the other players to plot his demise. During our evening of play, we witnessed Bill roll three Yahtzees in a single game. Rumor has it he once rolled five of them during a game, but that may be best left to legend. It was time to fall asleep to *Robin Hood* anyway.

*   *   *

Thursday morning there was enough time to have breakfast (including Waffles By Bill™) before leaving. The car was packed, and the bikes were strapped onto the trunk. Senator never did feel up to riding his, but at least

---

* acceptable as both a noun and verb; possibly also as an expletive in certain circumstances

his toe felt significantly better than when we left home. We vaguely recalled the doctor saying it could take six weeks or more to completely heal.

We enjoyed our last vacation conversation with our friends while watching the feeding frenzy outside. Within the span of their two-week stay, the birds and squirrels hit up Bill and Marge for enormous amounts of seed and suet. Like many other Door County residents, they know when it's tourist season. We finished our coffee and said our reluctant good-byes.

As is usually the case when you have spent a good part of your trip in the rain, the sun beamed brightly as we left. Driving home I was already looking forward to another trip. We did not leave Door County behind entirely, though. During a quick stop for gas, Senator emerged from the convenience store with his souvenir gift to me-- the official Door County Vacation Coloring Book. $4.00 bought a whole lot of joy on the way home.

Chapter 4
Climb Every Mountain, or At Least Attempt One: Late July 2014

Less than a week after returning home from Door County, we were packed and on the road once more. This time we were heading east. About four months earlier I was delighted to learn that if I played my finances right, we could take a short trip to Pennsylvania and New York, the object being to visit the Stoogeum and Sleepy Hollow/Sunnyside. The Stoogeum is, of course, a museum dedicated to all things Three Stooges. Sleepy Hollow Cemetery was the inspiration for Washington Irving's famous work, and Sunnyside was his home, both of which were located in Tarrytown, New York. Based on this light itinerary, and the calculated distance between Ambler, PA and Tarrytown, NY, we should have been able to accomplish said goals in five days. But you know me better than that by now.

It was late March when I began to reason that, as long as we were going east, we could also swing up to the Adirondacks and do some hiking. I had passed by the fringes of the mountains* a few times, but I had never spent any time hiking within them. I began the tedious process of researching many, many accommodations, which only ensued in general frustration. Either they were overpriced for what they offered, or they were already booked, as July fell in their peak travel season.

In the meantime, my brain began that familiar travel-junkie stream of consciousness that I have honestly inherited from both of my parents. *Huh... look at that... Valley Forge is actually sort of close to the Stoogeum. Might as well plan a stop there. What's that? A historic Gothic revival mansion just up the road from Sunnyside? Can't very well skip that. Come to think of it, as long as we've got to add an extra night to cover Valley Forge, it would be simply foolish not to break up the first day and plan a stop at Jean Bonnet Tavern.*

In addition to my scheming, Senator was slipping into the quicksand as well. "Michelle called the other day..." he began.

"Oh yeah? How're they doing?" I inquired about our friends from Brooklyn.

"Good. She says they are actually getting out of the city for a month or so. They are renting a place near Woodstock, in the Catskills, maybe? Anyway, she wants to know when we're coming for a visit."

---

* only by New York standards

Due to our unpredictable schedule and the fact that Spencer and Michelle were now parents of a three-year old, our visits had grown fewer and farther between. I had not planned on seeing them, but this was practically falling into our lap. When I pulled out the map-- yes, as the rest of the world strives for pocket-size digital information, I still prefer the sprawl on the family room floor method-- I confirmed that the route from Tarrytown, New York to the Adirondacks would go right past their destination. "Yep, put them on the itinerary. We can fit it in!" I announced, as the satisfied navigator.

Now back to the Adirondacks. Usually I enjoy each planning phase of a vacation, but it was becoming a chore. I was finding myself more interested in the other stops on the trip, as opposed to Lake Placid, where we had planned to spend the most time-- three days. A sane person would have considered the agenda and determined that there were now so many exciting things to experience that the Adirondacks could be dropped without regret. I, on the other hand, took a different course of action. Like a reasonable person, I dropped Lake Placid from the route. Like Wendy V, I proceeded to book five nights in the White Mountains of New Hampshire. After all, it was only six hours out of the way...

That is how our five-day excursion turned into a packed twelve-day adventure. The final itinerary vaguely resembled the one with which we had started, and I couldn't wait. It occurred to me that perhaps I had really just been looking for an excuse to go back to my beloved White Mountains all along. If so, I can accept that. What concerned me more, however, was the status of Senator's still-definitely-broken toe.

In classic Senator fashion, despite the fact that he had skipped any bike riding in Door County, he announced that he was determined to attempt a hike. Hhmmm. That could be a bit tricky in the state that invented the boulder. Time would tell. At least this time we would be in a car that I could drive, as opposed to taking his stick shift vehicle.

On a Tuesday morning in the middle of July, we packed last-minute items and loaded the car. As I was leaving our bathroom for the last time, I spotted a familiar but hideous creature on the wall. I was not about to let him* have the run of the house for the next week and a half, so I acted. SWAT!! One crumpled centipede was quickly transferred to the garbage on our way out. If there were any more, they were smart enough not to show their legs around me.

Soon we were breezing through Indiana, and soon we were reminded that tolls constitute a significant percentage of the budget when traveling east. I tried to put it into perspective, though. Relatively speaking, it was a small sum to pay to escape Illinois. Three hours later, I was once again digging out the cash as Ohio loomed on the horizon.

We were making good time, which fit my plans to take Senator to one of the very few restaurants that have ever interested us. Before that, however, I wanted to check into our reserved room. Online I had found a relatively

---

*   (or her; let's be fair)

new bed and breakfast with stellar reviews. The price was right, so I decided to give it a try. We parked our car in back and walked around to the street-side entrance. Stepping into the foyer, we could see that its high walls and hallway were very elegantly decorated in early Victorian style. A formal dining room was starting to fill with dinner guests.

I hoped that it wouldn't be too stuffy for our style, but I soon shed that concern. It took several minutes before someone greeted us. She seemed somewhat panicked, and had obviously been rushing around, based on her frazzled appearance. I explained that we had a reservation, hoping that I wouldn't later regret that fact. She ducked in back, and I could hear her murmuring something to a man. In a few moments he emerged, making apologies and immediately guiding us to our room.

The home was big, and due to it being a Tuesday night in a relatively new establishment, most of it was empty. The host explained that he had automatically upgraded us to larger suite. When he opened the door, I was almost overwhelmed. The ceilings seemed two stories tall. Though the room was spacious, it still seemed out of balance with such high ceilings. The combination made me look ridiculously small in the mirror, and it lent an unexpected echo to all of our words.

We only spent a few minutes in the echo-chamber, since we were ready for a bite to eat. The fruit we had eaten hours ago was no longer holding us, though all we had been doing was sitting on our butts all day. I am always amazed at how this happens. Once we were ready, we left our room and drove a few miles down the road.

In the sleepy town of Bedford, in southwestern Pennsylvania, stands Jean Bonnet Tavern. With a history older than the United States itself, this landmark stopover still provides dinner and drinks to weary travelers who walk (or stumble) into its thick stone walls. We ordered our pub grub and relaxed by the dim lantern light. Pewter blurred the reflection of candlelight, as our conversation fell off to simple contentment. I could tell it was going to one of my favorite trips to date. I just hoped Senator's foot would not cause him too much pain.

Back at the room we cleaned up and got into bed. For a moment I again stared at the far away ceiling and the floral wallpaper leading all the way up to it. Our room could easily have had a loft. Senator scrolled through the channels, eventually settling on an old *Honeymooners* episode. At home we have every episode of the brilliant landmark comedy, but that did not stop us from watching eagerly. Just as Ralph was about to send Alice "to the moon" yet again, I dozed off.

*   *   *

Wednesday morning we chose our table for breakfast in the empty dining room. There was a bright sun shining through the east window, sparkling through the glasses. We weren't sure if anyone even knew we were there, but in a moment a woman with a coffee pot came and filled our cups. She had a quiet demeanor, but she looked pleasant and content. She apologized, explaining that she had been sick the previous day, and was not able to greet us when we arrived, hence the confusion. She then excused herself to go get our breakfast.

It seemed funny to be eating alone in such a big room. The scale of everything there was much larger than it looked from the outside. We ate our eggs and muffins, and then downed the remainder of our juice and coffee. It was relaxing, be we had another stop a few hours east, so we checked out and hit the road.

Throughout Pennsylvania we had encountered numerous construction projects. Some were miles long. Others were shorter. Some fell somewhere in between, seemingly linking several smaller projects by brief, intermittent spells of open road. In almost every case, I was perplexed. Rarely were work zone speed limits posted. Sometimes we were instructed to slow down, but to what speed was anybody's guess. Starting and ending lines were vague as well. Sometimes we entered a construction zone, guided ourselves between dozens of warning signs and barrels, and then drove for miles without seeing any trace of orange. Apparently the work zone had ended, but there were no signs indicating so. Had they forgotten to tell us when to go fast again? Was it a speed trap? Should someone with out-of-state plates even dare to ask these questions?

The strange construction patterns continued most of the way to Valley Forge, but we still made good time. Even inside the park there was a short detour due to construction. At one point I thought we might even be in the wrong area, since the lot was mostly empty. Not finding any more activity elsewhere in the park, we decided we must be in the right spot. We parked the car and walked, slowly, to the visitor center.

Inside the theater, we received our Valley Forge 101 briefing. In 1777, under the expertise of General George Washington, Valley Forge was chosen as the military's winter encampment. Its relatively close proximity to Philadelphia would provide protection for the city, which was the largest in the colonies, boasting a population of 20,000. At the beginning of the endeavor, 12,000 hearty men set up camp, building small, crude log cabins in which to reside. While it was not the coldest encampment the army had ever known, it did not take long for disease and lack of essential supplies to claim the lives of about a quarter of the men.* Eventually, the Prussian soldier Baron Von Steuben stepped in to assist with the efforts. While the Americans were tough, he was appalled at their lack of 'professional' soldiering. In Europe, when he commanded the ranks, they acted. In these wild colonies, the troops demanded a reason for each order before obeying. In the end, Von Steuben's efforts and the army's cooperation paid off, and many lives were probably saved because of it.

From the visitor center we drove the winding roads throughout the park. At several points we stopped to walk the paved trails. One of these led to a few old soldier cabins. Twelve men once shared these quarters, which appeared to be about the size my modest living room. In this part of the park very large, old oaks-- perhaps

---

* According to the film in the visitor center, two diseases actually were *not* threats. There were no instances of smallpox because they could already inoculate for it. There was also no problem with scurvy, thanks to a sufficient (as least for medical purposes) supply of rum.

witnesses to the birth of the country-- stood just far enough apart to provide shady recesses between vast, grassy views.

Elsewhere in the park, the road climbed and circled around into deeper woods. It was a warm day, but the breeze and the cool forest held many inviting nooks and overlooks. Soon we found ourselves at an immaculately-tended two-story stone building, about the size of an average three bedroom home. The solid but unpretentious structure turned out to the be General Washington's headquarters. The inside consisted of a few simple rooms in which to eat, sleep, and plan strategy against one of the most powerful armies on Earth. Upstairs was a sparse loft, reached only by a steep ladder. It could have easily been just another farmhouse, which only added to the wonder of how the Americans ever managed to pull it off.

We enjoyed the grounds of Valley Forge National National Historic Park for a while longer, and then left to find our accommodations for the night. Though we were packing a lot into the trip, everything was aligned and timed in such a way that we never had to do an enormous amount of driving to reach the places we were staying. The overall pace seemed manageable. As we drove to our next bed and breakfast, however, I was beginning to question my planning.

What should have been a fifteen minute drive became one and a half hours and at least twenty blood pressure points. Traffic was moving swiftly; that was not the problem. I also did not think directions were the problem, since they only required hopping on Route 202 and taking a direct exit to the very road where the b&b was.

135

The trouble began when a road that ran north/south was marked east/west. Using my best judgment, I chose west. Before the east/west split actually occurred, the road we wanted appeared as an exit. Great! I wouldn't have to choose. Thus we took it, and ended up... nowhere near any bed and breakfast.

No harm done. We got back on the highway with the intention of trying to take the road the other direction. This only proved to redirect us back to where we started. It was like a maze, and nothing was lining up with the maps. Throw in an unmarked detour, and we were about to give up. Even technology let us down, as we were not able to access any internet connection to check online directions. Likewise, a phone call to the owners only resulted in a voicemail message. We then tried to buy a local map, but two gas stations and a convenience store did not sell any such item. I only had one more trick up my sleeve. What if we completely ignored the exit we had taken, (even though it had the exact name we were looking for,) then drove for a while longer, and randomly took the next exit if it looked like a road that could potentially lead to a historic residential district? Somehow, after watching the odometer click far too many miles for such a short distance, it worked. I really don't think we could find it again if we had to.

When we finally arrived at the home, one of the owners greeted us, explaining that his wife was not back yet. "Oh, I didn't expect you yet. You're an hour early." *Early?* Ah, yes, I had forgotten that I had given a later estimated time of arrival, so by some odd calculation, we were prompt. He pleasantly explained that they were in the middle of having the front stone steps repaired. As a result, we would have to take the side steps around to the veranda. No problem. The stairs were not bad to manage, and they stepped their way through ivy and other attractive foliage. I guess I had become engrossed in my surroundings, or just lost in the amazement of having actually found the place, because I failed to notice that I had stepped right over a garter snake on the way up the stairs. Wisely, Senator chose not to mention this fact until later. When he did, I was temporarily horrified, and watched the ground like a hawk any time we had to pass by that way. Ultimately, I guess what I didn't know didn't hurt me.

    We settled into our fourth floor room of what was officially deemed the oldest home in Pennsylvania. No other guests were staying there that night, and the owners lived two floors below. It was a very private retreat. Though our windows faced the road, the top of the house was obscured by trees, so it really felt more like we were in the world's most comfortable tree house. I did feel kind of bad about booking the top floor when I realized that Senator was still wincing occasionally, due to his broken toe. He never complained, though. He did, however, commandeer the small hallway refrigerator for his ice pack.

    As we were settling in, there was a knock at the door. The other owner had returned, and she wanted to make sure we had everything we needed. Or, she just wanted to talk. She was very friendly, especially when she learned that we were in town because we had gone to Valley Forge, and not the local casino. She proceeded to vent about guests who were more disposed to the latter form of entertainment than to historical points of interest. Then she moved on to expounding on local dining options. Before the conversation ended, she offered one last bit of enlightenment, after we happened to mention our difficulty in finding her home. "Oh, yeah," she said, with just a touch of mischief in her voice. "There are five different sections of Swedesford Road, and none of them connect." I didn't feel quite so dumb after that revelation. As a consolation prize, she gave us a copy of the locals' secret map.

Fully empowered with the hidden knowledge of how the main roads and back roads connected, we set out for a bite to eat. Senator hobbled down the stairs, and I apologized, mentally noting for the first time the fact that everywhere we would be staying was on at least the second floor. We stepped out to the 2nd story porch and walked around to the outside steps. This time we were both moving cautiously: he for his foot, me for slithering enemies. Happily, we made it to the car without incident.

We were not picky about where we ate, so we decided to try one of the suggestions of the innkeeper. She directed us to tavern that dated back to the mid-1700s, which promised to be a more meaningful experience than the local Pizza Hut. We dared to hope that, perhaps, we had stumbled onto another Jean Bonnet Tavern, complete with candles, heavy beams, and plenty of ubiquitous Pennsylvania stone. Alas, we were disappointed to find ourselves in just another too-hip metro/bistro/café with slow service and overpriced food. I'm not saying that serving my sweet potato fries in a parchment liner in a modern metal spiral cup didn't require creativity; I just didn't see it as 18th century authentic.

We finished our dinner, much to the dismay of our waiter, who was understandably disappointed in the fact that we were only drinking water. We were happy to leave our table with the view of the gas station for our bedroom, with the view of the trees and night sky. The temperature had dropped to a very comfortable summer evening low, allowing us to open the windows. We hardly ever heard a car... probably because no one else could find the place either.

*   *   *

Thursday morning we were up and ready to go early. Somehow our host knew exactly when we had stepped into the old kitchen. She magically appeared with a coffee pot a moment later. Our table was set for two, just a few feet away from a fireplace that had first warmed a family and cooked their meals over 300 years before. In Europe or Asia this may not be as impressive, but in America it is staggering. I couldn't take my eyes off of the giant kettles and the built-in ladder that once reached a loft where children and other items were stored.

We ate by candlelight*, chatting with our host about politics, local history, the economy, non-local history, and life in general. When the conversation rolled around to our plans for the day, she was stunned to learn that there was a

---

* While many have mastered the art of dining by candlelight, other meals should not be left out of this unique ritual. If the sun is ruining the mood, invest in heavy drapery.

museum fairly nearby of which she had not heard. While perusing a magazine a few years before, I had stumbled upon two sentences that grabbed the attention of this fan of classic comedy. Ambler, Pennsylvania, just north of Philadelphia, was the proud home of the world's only Stoogeum, a collection devoted solely to the work and lives of the Three Stooges. Indeed, I am one of the rare creatures who is both female and a raving Stooge fan. Our host was quiet for the first time since we had met her. She was trying to comprehend what a Stoogeum was, and how it had escaped her radar. I could already see the gears in her head working it into her local marketing spiel for her next guests.

We said good-bye and checked out, careful once more with wounded toes and those afraid of snakes. It was a beautiful home, and I would like to visit again someday. In the meantime though, the lure of pie fights and slapstick were calling. We were on our way to the Stoogeum at last.

In a half hour or so we reached Ambler. It was a small town, so as a Stooge fan I pictured the museum as the natural centerpiece. A large art deco shrine on the village green, with streets named after Moe, Larry, and Curly extending out from it seemed appropriate to me. Instead, we almost missed the nondescript building. Even though it was less than a block from the main road, it was modestly tucked behind some office buildings and what may have been condos. The outside of the building was fairly plain, with a black and white sign that simply read "The Stoogeum". Around the entrance were about ten parking spaces.

I still held high expectations. I had to; with only one

open-to-the-public day per week, I had basically planned our entire trip around the Stoogeum. After a few moments, a woman changed the sign and unlocked the door. Senator and I comprised exactly half of the crowd that had been eagerly awaiting entrance.

We paid our admittance (no checks), swore not to take photographs (don't even think about it), and walked upstairs to begin viewing the exhibits. Immediately it was worth the pilgrimage. Multiple galleries gave behind-the-scenes glimpses into the lives of Moe, Larry, Curly, Shemp, and yes, Joe Besser and "Curly Joe" DeRita. Photographs, handwritten letters, and even old tax returns told the story of one of America's favorite comedy teams.

Just as we were about to go downstairs, a life-sized replica of Moe, Larry, and Curly stood together, staring right at us. Standing at an average height of 5'4", it was a reproduction of the Three Stooges in bellhop uniforms from a scene in *Idle Roomers*. We continued down the staircase, which was surrounded by cartoon and literary references to the Three Stooges. When we reached the lower level, (which is quite a trick when you are walking while reading,) the hall opened up to a complete exhibit of lobby cards and movie posters. Next to that, thousands of toys, games, media clips, and more illustrated the broad influence the Stooges have had on pop culture for over eighty years.*

My head was swimming as we approached the art gallery. Various media in various sizes paid tribute to the

---

* To date, there even exists a Three Stooges craft beer. The tag line, of course: "We all put the yeast in!"

boys and their repertoire of escapades. It was a lot to take in, and the biographical information was staggering. We were having a blast, and there was still one final stop before we went on our way.

For those purists who want to escape the information overload and immerse themselves in total Stoogocity, there is the theatre, which plays nonstop Three Stooges shorts. We plopped ourselves down and indulged. If you thought Moe was crabby on your television or computer screen, you must experience his eye pokes and smacks on the big screen. In short, a private collector has put together a world-class, relatively new museum. (It probably didn't hurt that his wife was related to Larry Fine.) The museum's only drawback is its lack of publicity, but now that I've mentioned it in this book, they will probably have to open six hours per week, instead of five.

Leaving the Stoogeum, we traveled through several small towns in eastern Pennsylvania. It seemed that each of them had the same staples: cafés, gas stations, small grocery stores, and antique shops. The tranquility shifted a bit when we crossed over into New Jersey, joining the interstate. Fortunately, we were still far enough west to avoid Newark and New York City. Even being that far out, though, the traffic increased steadily as we approached the Tappan Zee Bridge*.

We were on our way to Tarrytown, New York, home of the legendary Sleepy Hollow Cemetery and plenty more. My original plan was to cross the Hudson and stay in or near the town, but rooms were sparse and far too pricey for

---

* or, "Zappan Tee" as Senator called it

what they offered. Though it would entail a few miles of backtracking Thursday afternoon and Friday morning, I booked a room on the west side of the Hudson, reasoning that a few $5 tolls were better than an extra hundred bucks for accommodations. As we drove onto the bridge, I noticed a delivery truck with the name "Van Tassel Cleaners" painted on the side. I took that as a good sign, and we proceeded west.

Senator and I had actually been to Sleepy Hollow Cemetery once before, on our first trip to the Big Apple. It was only the second time we had traveled together, and in a fit of mad passion or stupidity, we decided to rent a car and drive north out of the city to the small town. As expected, the traffic was tight for the whole ride up, but I still remember a flawless afternoon on the gently sloping mounds of the graveyard. The sun was shining, but the old hardwoods took care of me, providing shade along the avenues of the quiet little city. I had been wanting to repeat the experience, this time with Washington Irving's stories fresh in my mind.

Our second foray into the cemetery that was more alive with literature than it was with people, was a little different. The sky was partly cloudy, alternating between blazing patches and rain-swelled masses. Senator, who had insisted on doing most of the driving that day, decided that his still-wounded toes needed a rest. Thus, he pulled into Sleepy Hollow, found an unobtrusive side road, and propped his foot up on the dashboard. It was clear that I would be walking among the headstones alone. There was no safety concern, however, as a few families and small groups of tourists had invaded my sanctity. To their credit, they mainly meandered quietly around the most popular areas. I would have preferred solitude, but I could not be disappointed when I savored the view in every direction. Along the back side of the property ran the creek. All around were 18th and 19th century stones, mausoleums, and rusted iron gates. Down the hill was the solid and stately Old Dutch Church. Trees and bright red flowers filled in the gaps, while the Hudson's blue ribbon formed the horizon in the distance.

Drunk on the pleasure of being surrounded by nature and dead literary giants, I stumbled back to the car. Senator played it cool, but he could not resist taking some well-framed photographs; the opportunities were too vast. I chugged some water and tried to make it obvious to the wandering families that Senator and I were together. I was starting to think it might not look good that a single guy was parked alone in a graveyard, just sitting there with his camera.

We drove several more miles around the many looping roads of Sleepy Hollow. The sun had given up, yielding to a gray sprinkle that added mystery to the scene, even in daylight. I had had my graveyard fix, and Senator had rested a little while. Now we just had to shuffle our way back west across the Tappan Zee to our hotel.

Again traffic was heavy on the bridge and even heavier off of it. We drove several miles into areas that looked increasingly suburban, lacking any of Tarrytown's charm. After making a two-mile loop out of our way due to poor detour signage, we found ourselves at our hotel.

Thankful to be done with the major driving for the day, we parked and checked in.

Senator's foot was throbbing again, becoming a very present reminder that he still had a way to go before it was healed. Since Friday would be very busy, we opted for a quiet night. We unpacked only the essentials and flopped on the bed. With foot elevated, Senator called our friend Michelle, confirming that we were still on track schedule-wise. Though he assured her that we did not need to be entertained while there, she informed him that the four of us had plans for dinner and a small concert. *Okay, sounds fine.*

In the meantime, we were relishing the lack of activity. We had only to scrape ourselves together and drive a mile or so to find a bite to eat. Fortunately, a storefront restaurant nearby did a hopping homemade calzone business. Three or four young guys raced around the kitchen working dough, cheese, and other goodies together under the watchful eye of an old master. The phone rang endlessly while we waited for our order in the simple plastic booth. It took a while, but it was worth the wait (and weight) when we received the enormous mounds of Italian delight. Back at the hotel we really should have split one... but we didn't.

* * *

Friday morning we were up and out the door early. I was anxious to get to Sunnyside, Washington Irving's home, and I didn't know how tight the weekday morning traffic would be on the bridge. As it turned out, we coasted right through, unlike the previous afternoon. We again paid our toll and turned south after crossing the Hudson. Years ago I had been to Sunnyside, and I was looking forward to revisiting it with Senator. I remembered an unusual storybook cottage on secluded grounds with riverside views.

We arrived before they were even open, which seemed to slightly bother the ladies working in the gift shop. It was a beautiful morning, though, so we were content to roam the grounds for a while until our tour started. Then I realized why the guides were stressing. A group of grade schoolers poured out of a bus and filed down to the entrance. While I would have loved this type of field trip when I was nine, probably even wandering away from the group if given the opportunity, I failed to comprehend the lofty goal(s) the event's organizer(s) had in mind. These kids didn't know Rip Van Winkle from Ichabod Crane. They were clearly more interested in their juice boxes than the uniquely blended architecture of a home owned by America's Number One Knickerbocker.

I decided to get ahead of this thing and make sure our reserved tour time was not the same as that of the four-foot mob. When I went back into the gift shop for some sly research, I was immediately halted by a tour guide in period dress. "Are you with *that* group?" she demanded, no explanation of which group necessary.

"No!" I blurted out, probably a little too emphatically. "I was just checking the time for our tour. We have 10:00 tickets," I offered in defense.

"Oh, okay." She relaxed, slightly. "There are nine of you. You'll meet Joan right out there." With her hand she indicated a side door that led to a path. With her eyes she stared in exhaustion at the picnic tables outside the main door, now teeming with children. Gift Shop Attendant and I were friends again.

We quickly made our way outside, happy to join Joan while we waited for the others to navigate their way through the field trip chaos to join the adult tourists. There were three couples, including us, along with a set of grandparents and their chatty granddaughter, who looked to be about eight or ten.* Everyone was smiling and eager to begin. The granddaughter, whom her grandparents fancied to be nothing short of a genius, was more eager to enlighten us all with her extensive Sleepy Hollow knowledge. Now, had the child wanted to discuss how European travel influenced Irving's work, or why the man never seemed to find true love, I might have been inclined to engage in conversation. Instead, this girl, (who we were several times informed was visiting from California†) only spouted off random memories from movie renditions of Irving's stories. Once would have been cute. Twice would have been forgivable, eliciting polite nods from the group. After about the fifth time, however, Joan, who had been patiently giving her talk, was having none of it. She interrupted the brat. "Forget the movie; listen to me!" Everyone but the grandparents smiled. This is why I think all historic site tour guides should be New Yorkers.

The girl toned it down somewhat, but the

---

* Senator would say six... or fourteen. Is it weird that I find his complete lack of experience with children so attractive?
† that figured

grandparents were still hopeless. They persisted in asking stupid questions for most of the first half of the tour. No, I don't mean they were stupid questions because they should have automatically known the answers; they were stupid questions because Joan had just answered each of them during the previous ten minutes. It was like talking to four-year olds. Actually, maybe the granddaughter wasn't so bad, all things considered.

In between ignoring the threesome, we learned a lot about the strange home. Washington Irving moved there in his fifties, after securing his fortune. He incorporated lots of styles and lots of quirky angles into the design. No two rooms were alike, in contrast to most houses of the day. Provisions were made for ventilation that took advantage of the breezes coming off the river. A gravity-based system brought hot and cold running water into the home, fed by a nearby pond. At one point there was a lovely beach at the edge of the property, but the noisy, dirty trains put a stop to that in the 1840s. All in all, it must have been an idyllic setting for Irving, his brother, and his five nieces.

We concluded our tour, personally thanking Joan for a job well done on all counts. Bypassing the main path to the home, we walked the more remote areas of the property to a garden. We cut through it on our way to the parking lot, which was filling in quickly. Senator started the car, and I glanced at the time. Good, right on track. There was one more stop before leaving Tarrytown, just five minutes up the road.

While planning the Vacation That Kept Accidentally Growing, I had learned that Lyndhurst, a Gothic revival mansion, was also located near Sleepy Hollow. I did not know much about the place, except that it was large, ornate, and situated on sprawling grounds that overlooked the Hudson. Those were good enough reasons for me to reserve two tickets for a tour. It was sunny and dry, and the temperature was hovering in the mid-70s when we drove up the winding, tree-dotted lane to the estate. Since we were early, we had time to walk the property in the ideal weather.

We also had time to watch a documentary film in a room adjacent to the small gift shop. Both were located in a well-preserved building that was part of the carriage house and chauffeur's complex. From the film, I learned that there had only been three owners of Lyndhurst before it passed into the hands of the National Trust for Historic Preservation, allowing yours truly to explore its opulence in the full voyeuristic pleasure that only a home tour of a robber-baron could offer.* Yes, it was the third owner, Jay Gould, who would prove to be the most interesting and dubious of the succession.

Soon our tour guide met us, and only us. He was a little surprised, and we were delighted to find that we were the only ones who had signed up for the 1:00pm tour. Good-- we could focus on what we wanted to see, ask questions, and forgo time lost to the self-indulgent ramblings of a spoiled child. Up the hill we trotted, pausing at the grand entrance to the home.

Heavy blocks of solid marble framed the entire portico and foyer. Only it wasn't marble. While the owner

---

* Cigar, anyone?

of Lyndhurst at that time-- I believe Gould-- certainly could have afforded marble, he chose instead to import a fine artist who could paint an amazingly accurate faux marble finish on the walls. Why go through so much trouble for something fake? Simple-- because the process was actually more expensive that using real marble. When you are one of the wealthiest men on the planet, the object is not necessarily to obtain the best product; it is to spend the most money.

Our guide showed us the parameters of the original 7,000-square foot home, which the second owner enlarged to 14,000 square feet. (His family simply could not deal with being so cramped.) We continued through halls, galleries, and beautiful rooms which once contained beautiful people who could either sit on beautiful furniture or stand next to beautiful objects while they discussed whatever beautiful topics tickled their beautiful fancies. At every turn the wealth was astounding. A single painting in the library was valued at $15,000,000. The desk where Jay Gould conducted his railroad business was worth around $1,000,000.* On several occasions the neighbor guy had dropped off some glass trinkets, and even installed a few decorative windows. His name was Louis Comfort Tiffany.

Our entertaining guide continued with more details. He told us the home's guest list of regular visitors read like a roll call for early American literary greats. Edgar Allan

---

* As a point of reference, the computer *armoire* (French for a piece of furniture that looks like a closet and hides a lot of crap), at which I am currently sitting to write this, set us back about $80, including shipping.

Poe, Nathaniel Hawthorne, Washington Irving, and other writers all spent time at Lyndhurst. I was doing my best not to drool on the antique rug, which was probably cost more than my house.

One person who was distinctly *not* welcome at the home was railroad competitor Cornelius Vanderbilt.[*] In fact, Gould so despised Vanderbilt that he famously stated that he would "never step foot on Vanderbilt's property". This presented a challenge when Vanderbilt's railroad tracks separated Lyndhurst's main property from the adjoining waterfront access. Without river frontage, Gould could not take the preferred route to New York City. The problem was solved when Gould installed a bridge that ran up and over Vanderbilt's tracks, allowing the family to cross to the river without tainting even a toe. Well, what do you expect from a guy who printed counterfeit share certificates of his competitor's stock, in order to devalue it?

We wound our way through more rooms, each with loads of original furnishings, thanks to families who preferred to store rather than downsize. Finally our tour concluded in one of the outbuildings, which, no surprise, was the size of our yard. We thanked our guide and walked back to our car. We made one more loop around the property before taking Route 9 south toward the bridge. Once more across the Tappan Zee would take us to I-87[†], where we could head north to the Catskills.

It was late afternoon on a Friday, just an hour and a

---

[*] whose grandson, George Vanderbilt, built Biltmore Estate. (Say that ten times fast.)
[†] ironically, I-87 is an interstate located completely within one state

half outside of the biggest city in the nation. In other words, we were perfectly positioned to join the throngs of everyone else who thought they were escaping the urban masses. Even so, traffic buzzed along northward. Soon more trees and hills came into view as the sky clouded over. As we drove, I imagined how much fun it would be to spend a stormy night at Lyndhurst.

We followed our friend Michelle's directions toward the small town of Woodstock. Roads were dark, serpentine, and poorly signed. While we did not encounter any epic rock festivals, a significant portion of Woodstock's population were definitely aging hippies, which tend to fall into two categories. The first are the die-hards, who have not cut (or likely washed) their hair since the Nixon administration. They are still thumbing rides on the outskirts of town, although the dog that trots along beside them has been replaced a few times over the years. The second kind are the ones who took a detour. I don't mean they ended up at Altamont; I mean they tried the lifestyle of The Man for awhile. During this period of their lives, they actually managed to eke out a sustainable living, and not just on nuts and berries. They amassed reasonable wealth, retired, and now have sufficient disposable income to manage overpriced shops that sell colorful, useless glass baubles to tourists who haven't already spent all of their money at the painted rock shops or organic cafés across the street. Woodstock is filled with both varieties of hippie.

We eventually turned a corner into the woods and saw our friend waving while she was walking up from a clearing. We followed Michelle back to the house that she and her husband Spencer were renting for part of the summer. There we settled in among their dog, their nanny, and especially their three-year old son, Zimmerman, whose words-per-minute and activity level would shame a hummingbird's fervor. As we reintroduced ourselves to him-- it had been over a year since he had seen us-- he continued constructing his elaborate New York skyline out of blocks. In between giving us a tour of his Little Apple, he recited various letters of the alphabet, giving examples of words that could not exist without them. Edutainment indeed.

After visiting for a while at the house, Senator, Spencer, Michelle, and I ventured out to a very crowded restaurant. We chose outdoor seating, which seemed like a good idea on a mild summer night. Unfortunately, the air was calm and the service was quite slow, giving the mosquitoes ample time to feast on us. That was okay. We had enough laughs while reminiscing to set the tone for a fun evening ahead. Michelle had reserved tickets for an acoustic singer/songwriter concert in a small venue. The next time the server made the rounds, we paid our bill and left.

Inside the busiest few blocks of the town was an old hotel, whose main lobby area had been turned into a lounge that could hold about fifty people. Looking around, it seemed like thirty of them had forgotten to come. It was an interesting space, though. A vintage poster proudly boasted the building's fire-proof innovations. We took our seats in the dim room and waited for the show to begin. It might be worth noting that out of the corner of my eye I could see a little beagle puppy. He was leashed, and at the other end was a bleached blond woman, looking dopey and happy, and maybe a few other dwarves' monikers.

I won't say who we were there to see, because the blond figured in. I will say that the headliner was a man who had written several pop hits in the 1980s. He stood on stage looking somewhat haggard, but grateful to be there... or anywhere. His first several songs all followed the same depressing pattern-- very few chords, all weak, and all accompanying his own dreary, oddly-intoned vocals. I love a good melancholy dirge as much as the next gothie, but these were just plain sad. If he wanted to perform something somber, he needed about 300 tutorial sessions with Simon and Garfunkel in order to learn how to do it right. For a songwriter who looked to be in his mid/late 60s, I expected more than lame tunes about relationships gone bad and girls who just hung around the Pacific Ocean.

In short, it was like sitting through a Saturday Night Live sketch, only it was not supposed to be funny. Our eight eyes wandered from the stage, to each other, and then down to our laps, where we tried to compose ourselves. It didn't help that Michelle, upon recognizing one particular song she liked, blurted out a loud "Wooo!" To be fair, she wasn't trying to attract attention, but everything subtle becomes loud when only twenty people are in the audience. Tears started to squeeze out of the corner of my eyes as I spread my hand across my mouth and nose. I vowed not to look at Senator; it would have sent me into hysterics.

Finally the singer moved to break the monotony. He

invited a guest performer onto the stage with him, graciously thanking her for all she had done for him.* Sure enough, it was the blond. She took a few minutes to come forward, as she had to maneuver tying up her puppy and wrestling into her guitar strap. For reasons that were never justified, she took another moment to pretend to tune.

Like her counterpart, she was off-key and maudlin. Unlike him, she had a high, squeaky, childlike voice. She started to sway as she sang, "No-bod-y knows where my Jooooohn-ny has gooooone, but Juuuuu-dy left the same tiiiiime...." Yes, it's true. I didn't even try to hold back my laughter at this point. It takes real talent to turn *It's My Party*† into a funeral march. In fact, it took double the talent, because they both joined in, sharing the disharmonic misery.

Spencer was shaking and squinting into his hand. Senator was cringing, an interesting combination of annoyance and amusement. Michelle, who to this point had been the most supportive representative of our foursome, even gave up. Though we were in the last row, I'm sure others heard our snickers. All that was missing was for the beagle to start howling.

When the show finally ended, we made a quick exit to the foyer. In another moment we were in the car, where an hour and a half's worth of gaffaws came out in full force. The performance left much to be desired, but it was worth the price of admission for the satisfaction that only incurable laughter can bring. Then again, I can say that; I'm

---
* Perhaps she was his AA buddy(?)
† made famous in 1963 by Lesley Gore

not the one who paid for the tickets!

Back at the house we retold our experience to the nanny. In case she felt left out, we each volunteered various impersonations of the performed songs. We all visited for a while longer, lingering over our coffee. Finally it was time to retire, with only the sounds of the dark, lonely woods outside.

*   *   *

Saturday morning was low-key. Spencer made French toast for everyone, and we chatted for a while at the table. We only had the morning to spend with our friends, since we would soon be on the road again. They had other activities as well, so we spent our last hours together casually in one of the neighboring towns.

We got into our friends' car, this time with their son, too. It was a lovely, wooded, curvy ride to the town, narrated in full detail by Zimmerman. I am still astounded by both the quantity and quality of his 3-year old vocabulary. At one point we passed an old graveyard. He excitedly pointed out, "Look, tombstones! We need to go!" This was a kid I could relate to. (I basically do the same thing when Senator drives.)

We stopped in the local bookstore to poke around for a while. With the mountains on my mind, I went straight for the travel section. Nothing particularly grabbed my attention, but it was still the perfect place to spend a cloudy Saturday morning. We then stopped by a buzzing farm market. It was packed with people eager to see what was fresh this week, and even more eager for free samples. One stand sold maple suckers, which Senator deemed the appropriate snack to prepare for a drive through Vermont into New Hampshire.

Our time together had already come to an end, but a brief visit was better than no visit. We drove back to the house and said good-bye to our friends. After only a quick stop inside to grab our bags, we were on our way. I could hardly believe I would spend that night in New Hampshire.

With each hour behind the wheel, the scenery shifted a little more. New York was soon behind us, and we crossed into Vermont. About halfway through the drive we stopped by a roadside stand for some coffee. Like most Vermonters, the owner was accommodating, and just friendly enough to take the edge off of her suspicions about us. Not hide them, mind you-- just take the edge off. The coffee was hot and rather good. More importantly, it sufficiently fueled Senator to drive us the last stretch to The Granite State.

We entered New Hampshire from a different highway than we had last time, and I think I liked it even better. Then again, I have not seen a bad side to the state yet. Turning up the familiar street, we parked in the lot of The Wilderness Inn, where we had stayed two years before. This is a rarity for us. Unless we are visiting people, we normally explore new places each time we travel. I was so taken with the area, though, that it was an easy decision to go right back to it. Seeing the Whites close by, I felt zero remorse at skipping the Adirondacks.

We checked in, happy to see that absolutely nothing had changed, including the delicious breakfast menu that we would attack for the next several mornings. We did not stay in our room very long, because we were eager to kick off our Saturday night amid the romance of the laundromat. Like so many tasks which would be a chore at home, this one was fun because it was occurring while on vacation. In fact, thanks to proper timing, we were able to dump the dirties in the wash, order pizza to go, switch the load to the dryer, and enjoy our pizza in the car, under the emerging stars.

We folded our jeans, tee shirts, sweatshirts, and other vacationwear. I was extra careful not to drop the clean undies on the floor. Incidentally, I always picture laundromats as crowded places, but if you want the joint to yourself (or in this case, yourself and your date,) try a Saturday night, especially in northern New Hampshire. Heck, if we ever moved there, I might be content to spend a lot of Saturday nights this way.

When we had restocked the suitcases, we drove the mile back to our room. We were staying in the same small but cozy room that we had stayed in the last time. In my mind it was ours. I almost convinced myself that no one had stepped foot in it since the last time we were there. Maybe they changed the sheets or refilled the toilet paper, but that was it. Like a temporary squatter, I mentally claimed the space for our domain during the next several days. I then drifted off to the dull red glow of my travel clock and the sound of Senator lightly snoring next to me.

*   *   *

Sunday morning we trotted down to breakfast in the sunny enclosed porch, like we owned the place. I don't mean we were rude or demanding; we just belonged there. As we sat down to juice and coffee with a mountain view, we started to plot our day. Ultimately, Senator's still-ailing foot would choose the agenda. Though he was determined not to miss out on our hiking plans, we decided it was best to ease into the mountains. Consulting the Wendy V Master List, we chose several low-intensity activities.

Before heading out to the woods, we made one essential pit stop. Somehow we had not made it to the White Mountains Visitor Center the last time, though we were, in fact, White Mountain visitors. It was now time to undergo the ritual. We browsed a few displays on local flora and fauna and read the weather and trail updates. Naturally, I increased my wardrobe by two New Hampshire sweatshirts.* Senator then added a cd to my pile at the cash register. "Want this?" he asked, already having decided on the purchase.

"Of course!" How had I existed this long without the Kancamagus Highway driving tour audio narration? As we waited for the visitor center employee to finish answering a phone call, we could detect the questions with which the poor woman had to contend. When she was finally able to escape the caller, she vented her exasperation to us. I was satisfied that she spoke to us as though we were locals. It seems that the party on the other end needed information regarding, but not limited to:

"Which hotel is closest to the attractions?" [Answer: Which attractions? The White Mountains encompass a significant portion of the state, with dozens of attractions

---

* Live Free or Die!

spread around the area.] "How long does it take to climb White Mountain?" [Answer: Hiking times vary greatly based on such factors as physical shape, skill, experience, weather, season, etc. Since, however, there is no "White Mountain", it should not take very long.] "Can I just walk from my hotel?" [Answer: Which hotel? To where? A typical drive around the main loop through the mountains can easily take two and a half hours. Actually, on second thought, yes, *you* should walk.] "How late are you open?" [Answer: We're not. This is a recording. In fact, the entire northern portion of the state is closed until further notice, or at least until tourist season ends.]

At least, that is how I would have answered, given some of the silly questions. I might also suggest that the person look into that information terminal that seems to be catching on across the country-- the "world wide web" I believe the kids are calling it.

From there it was a short drive to Lincoln Woods. We were glad to learn that, despite being surrounded by a mountain range, there are actually multiple options for trail grades. Whereas we had hiked heavily rooted, steep trails the last time we were in New Hampshire, we found that the Lincoln Woods trail was flat and relatively clear of roots and branches. Due to its easy terrain, and the fact that it links up with other long-distance trails, we encountered quite a bit of traffic on the trail, but it was pleasant, and still not what a Chicagolander would call crowded.

Senator enjoyed his walk, and he planned to do more each day, but in the meantime he needed something a little less active. We were entertaining the idea of kayaking on one of the many lakes in the area, so we drove to a secluded one that the owner of our bed and breakfast had recommended. We were just stopping to check it out, but it was more crowded than we had anticipated, so we left. We would have to find another lake some other day that was both 1.)ignored by the guidebooks, and 2.)uninteresting to locals.

On our way back to the main road, we stopped at a graveyard. It was sunnier and more open than I prefer, but the selection of old stones was not to be ignored. In a repeat performance of Sleepy Hollow, Senator elevated his foot while I explored. In particular, I searched for ones that pre-dated 1800, as these are virtually nonexistent in the Midwest. Too bad Zimmerman wasn't there to enjoy it with me.

Since Senator's extensive walking was done for the day, we opted to spend the remainder of the afternoon on a driving tour of some of the small towns in the region. Years ago I had done one of those online surveys that asks dozens of questions about your ideal living environment. While I usually don't bother with such questionnaires, this one was well constructed, and it delved into a lot of detail. In the results, one of the towns recommended for me was Littleton, New Hampshire. Ever since then I had been curious about it, so we took Route 3 northward.

On the way through the Franconia Notch region, there are multiple turn-offs for trail heads and points of interest. One of these leads to Boise Rock, which is a large boulder that once protected a fortunate (or unfortunate, depending on perspective) traveler who was caught in a blizzard. It, in itself, is mildly interesting, but of supreme importance is the naturally flowing well across the road from it. The last time we were in the area, I had ignored it, assuming that it was just a run-off fountain. This time Senator went over for a closer look. Next to it there was a sign explaining the source and inviting hikers to partake of the potable water. With a prayer to kill any vicious parasites, we filled our water bottles. "Well, this will either be very good or very bad..." I mused. As it turned out, it was the best water either of us had ever had, anywhere. Even for a state known for clean water, it was surprising. Senator was so impressed that he practically agreed to retire in New Hampshire based on the water alone. I wish I had a glass right now...

Littleton's main street has the reputation of being one of those stereotypical New England icons. The online pictures show attractive, carefully preserved buildings, on either side of a wide, tree-lined street. In a different part of the small town are the modern conveniences, including the ubiquitous box stores. Naturally, violent crime is unheard of, and residents rate their overall satisfaction with the area with high marks.

On a weekend afternoon in mid-July, however, Littleton's charms go unnoticed as the alert driver must navigate the very busy blocks of the main historic drag through town. It was as pretty as the pictures suggested, but it felt claustrophobic. Thus, my fantasies of living and teaching in Littleton were chilled. That was alright; there were more towns to explore.

On we drove to Bethlehem. Basically, it is a smaller,

quieter version of most of the mountain towns. It essentially contained lots of flowers, lots of trees, some respectable homes, a casual golf course, and not a lot of people. In fact, the most action Bethlehem sees is during the weeks leading up to the holidays, when folks flock to the local post office to have their Christmas cards marked from Bethlehem. I thought for a moment what it would be like to spend winter in the White Mountains. With Senator, our books and music, a hearty supply of food, and plenty of wood for the stove, I think I would relish it. We agreed that Bethlehem could be near the top of the 'someday' list.

We continued through a few more towns, villages, and rural areas. All of them had pleasing points, and none of them made me miss Illinois. As we drove back south toward our bed and breakfast, I scanned the woods for moose or bear. We were moving too fast, though, so I redirected my attention to the long-distance views of the range around Franconia Notch.

We made one more stop before going to our room. When in the North Woodstock/Woodstock area,* it is necessary to make a pilgrimage to Fadden's General Store. Along with the expected necessities for Northwoods survival, there is plenty of maplenalia. (If you think maple syrup is only for pancakes, you have led a sheltered life.) You can also find gift-y stuff at Fadden's. Pretend you are buying it to bring back home to someone, but feel free to

---

* I still can't get a clear reading on where one ends and the other begins, or, for that matter, why it appears that North Woodstock is south of Woodstock. I invite locals to contact me at their soonest convenience.

keep it for yourself. After all, can you really have too many dessert-fragranced soy candles?

It was only a few more blocks to our room, so we took a break for a while. Senator rested his foot, giving it a pep-talk for the days ahead, when he hoped to hike for longer periods of time. I was still doubtful as to the safety or wisdom of pushing it. In the meantime, we had another objective to tackle.

As twilight edged in, we deemed it a good time to grab some take-out food for the first official moose stake-out of the trip. For the event we found a small, empty parking lot that bordered the woods. Through the woods we could see a wide stream. We reasoned that it was a lovely spot for us to enjoy dinner, so why not for a moose? We watched and waited. Though there were plenty of green, slimy, and presumably delicious plants, no moose took the bait. Admitting defeat, we started the car and pulled onto the Kanc.

There was just enough time to claim our spot in the parking lot across from a resort. As we learned the last time, that particular resort sets off fireworks every Sunday night during the summer. Guests can see them up close. Freeloaders like us can see them from the comfort of our vehicle, surrounded by several other people with the same idea. One by one the rockets soared up, bursting into colorful explosions that echoed through the valleys. When the last streaks of the grand finale had faded, we left the lot and went back to our room. Our first full day in the mountains had exhausted us.

*   *   *

Monday was designated waterfall day. Though I have seen many waterfalls in my years of hiking and camping, I have always wanted to reserve a single day entirely for visiting several of them. Now that day had arrived. Senator still wanted to push his limits, so it seemed like a good compromise to make several smaller treks instead of one longer one. There were scores of falls to choose from, but I had narrowed the list down to four, ignoring ones we had already seen and focusing on the ones that sounded the most unique. Of course, I did not waste vacation time planning the excursion; this was all done ahead of time, probably when I was supposed to be working on lesson plans. Well, it was some sort of lesson, anyway.

We started out going east on the Kanc, and then north to the tiny village of Jackson. Conveniently, the falls ran along one of the roads in town, making them very easy to find. There the water is very wide, and the falls are gentle, very gradual tiers. The banks are flat and easy to walk around, which makes them an ideal spot for a picnic. We did not eat there, but we did nose around the many painters who had set up their easels to capture different angles of the falls. It was enticing and refreshing, but it also made us eager to move on to more remote falls.

Heading into the Pinkham Notch area, we stumbled onto a large base camp and visitor center. From there, hikers could take various trails up into the mountains. Some would splinter off, and some would eventually lead up to Mount Washington, the granddaddy of New England's peaks. We made a quick stop in the lodge to check the giant table map.

When we came back out, we began our ascent. Senator took his time, as it was the first uphill walking he had done since the break. Surprisingly, he soon picked up his pace. Unlike the flat Lincoln Woods trail, we were now back among the familiar roots and boulders. After about a mile, we reached an accessible part of Crystal Cascade. From the bridge, we had an excellent view of the clear, swiftly moving water. It was not a straight drop, but it was quite steep.

Leaving the bridge, we found a nook where we could sit on rocks near a pool. It was sunny, but not too warm-- ideal hiking weather. Since we wanted to see other falls, we resisted the urge to go further up the mountain. That was when Senator discovered that stepping down can be trickier than climbing up. Slowly we descended...

Eventually we made it back to the lodge. After pausing for a quick snack, we were on the road again. This time we would visit falls that were more secluded. According to my research, it would involve a lot of stairs. I hoped this would not be as difficult as going down a sloped trail, but Senator gave the nod of approval.

We found a spot in the small parking lot and looked around for the trailhead. Off to the side there was a subtle path that led across a road to what looked like weeds. From there, however, things got interesting. The path turned sharply, leading down a small canyon. For almost the entire walk, a roaring waterfall, several stories high, plummeted to the river beneath. This was a movie waterfall-- one you had to shout over to be heard, and one whose mist dampened your clothes and mangled your hair.

    Senator actually got to the bottom before me, which I took as an encouraging sign. I paused at one of the switchbacks to take picture of him. His back was to me, and it was only after I had finished the descent that I realized what he was doing. With a look of sheer bliss on his face, he was soaking his bare foot in the rushing water. He had accidentally found an excellent therapy for his foot. It was the best it had felt since he broke the toe. Score one more for the White Mountains. We basked inside the waterfall's spray and healing foot bath for a while longer, and then left to continue our tour.

    Because we happened to be driving past it, we next stopped at the Cog Railway's base station. The Cog Railway, as you may have already imagined, is a railway that propels travelers along a cog system. This allows it to climb at an eyebrow-raising 25% grade on average. (At its steepest, the grade reaches over 37%.) People have been taking this "railway to the moon"[*] to the summit of Mount Washington since 1869. I have not been one of those people, and even if it is around for another 150 years, I am not likely to be one of them. For one, we intend to someday hike to the top, rather than ride. More importantly, I don't even like to lean back in a recliner, let alone experience the helplessness of lying halfway back as someone else clunks me up a mountain. No thanks, and especially not for $68.00

---

* In the 1850s, when Sylvester Marsh first presented his idea for a railroad to the top of Mount Washington to the New Hampshire legislature, they scoffed, saying that he "might as well build a railway to the moon".

a pop.

At the base station, there really was not much to see. A few people milled around, but no trains were arriving or disembarking. We glanced at some stands filled with tourism brochures. The slots were filled with enticements to places we were skipping in lieu of nature's superior attractions. It wasn't a waste of time though; the bathrooms were immaculate.

By this point Senator had fallen under the spell of finding another waterfall basin in which to soak his foot, so we made another aquatic stop at The Basin.[*] Here fresh water swirled around in shallow, partially shaded pools. Brave people dipped their feet into the icy water. A few crazy kids even swam in it. I just enjoyed the fact that, unlike our rivers and streams at home, you could see straight to the bottom, several feet below. If it wasn't for all of the feet, it would have been tempting to drink it.

We left The Basin and returned to The Room.[†] There we lay around until hunger overpowered laziness. At home, we rarely go out to eat, generally preferring the quality and taste of homemade food. To try to preserve this habit somewhat while on the road, we sometimes peruse local nearby stores for portable picnic dinners. This is how we found ourselves roaming the local Price Chopper. Who says we don't know about night life? Two kinds of cheese, some crackers, a few pieces of produce, and a box of plasticware later, we had our dinner in the comfort of our car, with the woods and sunset for our tableside view. I

---

[*] actual name
[†] not actual name

guess we do like eating *out* after all.

It had been a long day, and we wanted a relaxing evening before tackling our most ambitious post-toe break hike. By 8:00pm we were in pajamas, sucked into a documentary on the history of the British Royal Family. We leaned a lot, most of which I have forgotten. I do recall that somewhere in Europe there is a monument that is supposed to be a solemn memorial. Instead, everyone just thinks it's ugly. Cheerio!

*   *   *

If you can walk an hour along a flat, easy path, and then you successfully navigate your way around several waterfalls, it stands to reason that you should, on the next day, attempt a three-hour mountain trek. At least, that is how Senator figured it. We had two more full days in New Hampshire, and he wanted to climb one of the 4,000-footers before we left the area. I couldn't disagree. I had carefully chosen the route for Mount Jackson/Mount Webster two months earlier, and I was looking forward to the challenge. That was before his tussle with the amp, however. After that, I had written off that part of the itinerary. He was insistent, though, so I dug through my notes and found the annotated trail map.

After a hearty, homemade breakfast under a party sunny sky, we drove to the trailhead. We double-checked our pack supplies and cell phone. Supplies were sufficient. Phone, as expected, had zero reception. We shrugged it off, relaced our hiking boots, and trudged through tall grasses into the woods.

It was slow going-- a few young children and a man

in his seventies passed us-- but we were moving forward. Beyond the trees we could hear yet another waterfall, and the air temperature was perfect for hiking. Senator took his time alternating between forward climbing, side-stepping around roots, and telling me to stop asking if he was okay. Eventually I did, for a while anyway.

In less than half an hour we were at Elephant Head, a boulder that opened up from the trail to a view of the valley below. In the valley sat the Victorian train station and platform. We were very comfortable as we sat enjoying the expansive vista and the upward drafting breeze. In fact, it became clear that if we had not made a move shortly thereafter, we might never have left.

Departing the short Elephant Head detour, we rejoined the main trail, which quickly spiked in slope. Our hike had morphed into a half-walk/half-climb. Senator was not only cautiously watching his steps; he was cautiously planning his grasp so as not to rely on the support of pushing upward from his left foot. It had suddenly become complicated. I was not able to help him, and he was not able to help me. It was every flatlander for himself/herself. In New Hampshire, they have a way of subtly taking your trail out from under you and replacing it with a vertical wall of spilled boulders. They call this a 'scramble', as in 1.)you have to scramble to get your butt up and over it, or 2.)you better scramble your butt out of there if you see one start to go.

In the end, we navigated the trail/scramble for about another half hour or so before stopping. The distinction of what was trail had all but disappeared. Senator sat about twenty feet beyond me, perched at a slightly higher elevation. I could tell his pain had started again, and we were both sweating quite a bit. It was clear to us that it was time to turn back. The mountain had won. It had been worth the effort, though. We saw more of the incredibly unspoiled beauty of the White Mountains, and frankly, it would have bugged us if we didn't at least try. Senator resolved the situation by vowing to climb a mountain the next time we visited the area. Naturally, he specified that it had to be the highest one.

As we drove around the Presidential Range, we listened to our $5 audio tour cd. Realizing we were on one of the narrated sections of highway, we jumped ahead to the track that told the story of the Russell-Colbath House, in front of which we found ourselves parked. It seems that Mr. Colbath once left the homestead, telling his wife he would be back "in a little while". Forty-two years later, he returned, surprised to find that, though the neighborhood hadn't really changed-- there still wasn't one-- his home life had. Specifically, there was no longer a Mrs. Colbath. There was, however, a nice, flat, ½-mile loop trail around the piney property. Senator took my hand, and we casually walked it, grateful that there were no hard scrambles, and grateful that neither of us had any plans to take a forty-two year walk.

We situated ourselves back into the car, deciding to let the tour cd determine our next location. We were certainly getting our five bucks' worth, as it directed us to another great spot, associated with another bizarre story. Rocky Gorge is a section of the Swift River with more cold, quickly moving, clean water. Senator's foot greatly appreciated this fact. In the part where we were, people could wade or even swim, but the current dances you around a little too strongly for my liking. Rocks provide stepping stones around the small river basin, but they terminate at a drop-off for which the spot is named. I won't retell the strange tale here, but your homework is to look up the event surrounding Rocky Gorge. Then you, too, will understand why swimming is strictly forbidden beyond a certain point.

Since there was still plenty of time before sundown, we treated ourselves to a completely out-of-the-way drive back to the flowing well at Boise Rock. The water was as pure and satisfying as when we tried it a few days before, so we filled up our bottles and indulged. I realize, Reader, that you might wonder why you just spent money on a travelogue that spends time extolling the merits of great spring water, but if you could taste it, you would understand. Until edible/drinkable books are a reality in the mass market, I can only offer this: the water at Boise Rock tastes like the pictures on every brand of bottled water try to make you believe they will taste. Confused? Just grab some empties and head to the White Mountains.

It was past dinner time. As was the unspoken routine, we grabbed some food and drove to a quiet spot on the edge of a forest. Car dinners can be tricky logistically,* but they can be so rewarding, even when the wildlife seems to be avoiding you at all cost. Try it at least once. Maybe you will be lucky enough to have some inhabitants of the

---

* Tip: I do not recommend including cole slaw on the menu.

forest come out to investigate.

We spent the remainder of the night plotting our last full day in New Hampshire. Since we would not be conquering any more mountains on this trip, we decided to take the opposite approach and head for the ocean. After all, there was only one state in between us and the Atlantic. If we started early enough, we could take our time meandering through quaint* towns on our way to the coast. Then we could follow the edge of the continent down, pausing whenever we felt the urge to stop at old bookstores or visit a beach. Head east, then south. Simple. Goodnight.

*   *   *

Wednesday morning was sunny, dry, and gently becoming warmer. It promised to be a great day to take a ride that would culminate with a walk along a Maine beach. In retrospect, it was very fitting that at the last minute we added yet another state to the route. This trip had been growing and evolving ever since I was naïve enough to plan a modest five day journey.

We ate quickly, checked that we had everything for a day-long excursion, and set out east along our favorite highway. For the most part, traffic was light as we drove through various small towns in eastern New Hampshire. Even though we had maps and understood how to interpret distance, I was still surprised at how fast we met the Maine border. That was a bonus; we would have more time at the ocean.

The plan was to follow some two-lane highways

---

* I hate that adjective. Don't you?

through the center of the state, and then drop down along the coast until we reached Portland and Kennebunkport, which I had remembered liking from our very first trip together in 2003. Again the routes were easy to follow, but the traffic gradually increased. Though the interior towns were still attractive for the most part, they lacked some of the laid-back charm of the northern New Hampshire towns and the seafaring culture of the southern coastal towns. I was a little disappointed, but we were still anticipating a fun afternoon once we arrived at our destination.

As it turned out, the fun was not to be had. Traffic became even more congested, relegating us to a frustrating pace. Rather than looking at people's homes and small businesses at 20mph, we decided to take the interstate until we were further south. Generally this is a simple feat. In this case, construction detours, confusing interchanges, and an inefficiently laid-out downtown conspired to waste another precious hour of our day. We could not see the ocean, or anything particularly scenic. Neither were there any sea breezes floating through the car. Our comfortable northern summer day had shot up to 90°F, forcing us to keep the windows up and the air conditioner cranked.

This was not the Maine I remembered. Where were the quiet villages and lobster shacks? Where had all these people come from? Most importantly, why did the car thermometer now read 93°F? The illusion was fading fast.

In a ditch effort to rescue some aspect of our afternoon, we exited the highway and turned down a road that looked promising. It was somewhat isolated, but we could see an open expanse of ocean. Sea grasses and sand were encouraging sites as we drove further. Finally, we reached an extremely well-kept neighborhood on the edge of the ocean. Old traditional Maine homes painted in tasteful muted hues depicted a simpler era. Friendly children rode bikes, people walked on sidewalks in front of their picket fences, and all seemed right with this light and breezy little corner of the world. I guess that's why we weren't allowed in.

We had found a sample of what we had been searching for, but access was restricted to residents only. No parking was available, and it probably would have meant getting ticketed if we did find a spot, so we drove a few sneaky loops through the area and then left. At least we had seen the ocean, tease though it was.

At this point, the family meeting jointly approved a change of objective. First, find a bathroom. Second, get the heck out of Maine and back to the White Mountains. At least we weren't lost... exactly. Because we were now back on the state highways instead of the interstate, we found ourselves among several small, privately owned establishments. Apparently none of these had public restrooms. It was great that we could purchase all of the souvenir stuffed animals, wind chimes, and themed coffee mugs we wanted, but not so great that we couldn't pee.

Eventually we came to a grocery store. Like a lighthouse in a hot, humid parking lot, it beckoned us. Inside we found very friendly staff members who directed us to the desired accommodations. It meant winding our way through the shipping and receiving department in the rear of the store, to the bewildered looks of a few employees, but we finally found a bathroom. The single-toilet room was clean and even had a lock on the door, unanimously making it the highlight of the afternoon.

We finished our business and bought some coffee for Senator to drink on the road.* Truth-in-advertising failed, as the paper cup showed a content moose wandering around a presumably local forest. Senator sipped and I sighed. Thankfully it was a short drive to the main interstate. We gladly paid the escape toll and fought for our spot among the on-ramp mergers. The next two hours were spent accepting defeat by breaking the speed limit. I would like to euphemize the day by calling it an impromptu adventure, but the truth is that it was just a waste of time. Senator had not even been able to dip his toe into the water.

By the time we reached our bed and breakfast, we were hungry. The sun was low in the sky, but we had enough time to pick up some calzones and locate a secluded picnic spot. Cheese oozed over the dough, as we performed the balancing act required by eating Italian food in a car. We relaxed and rolled the windows down to enjoy the twilight air. I wished we had spent the day hiking in the vicinity, but at least now I knew not to take any back routes through Maine if I wanted to see the ocean.

We finished our dinner and sat quietly for a while. I could tell Senator was thinking about the next project

---

* This is always a signal of two converging factors. The first is that Senator is getting tired, but because he still wants to drive, he requires the guaranteed stimulus of caffeine in his system. The second is that Senator has had enough. No questions asked.

awaiting him at home. I was doing the opposite-- trying *not* to think about what I had to do. We were both tired, so we wrapped up the leftovers and our mobile picnic. Cleaning up, stretching out on a soft bed, and watching mindless cable shows sounded pretty good right about then.

*   *   *

Thursday morning we packed up everything, relinquishing the claim we had temporarily staked on our corner of the house. We trotted down to breakfast one final time. I'm never hungry when I get up, but the appeal of a mountainside table and homemade cranberry syrup on anything are an alluring combination. I drank it all in, along with my last cup of decent coffee before reaching home. When it was time to go, we thanked our wonderful hosts, hoping we would get at least one more opportunity to stay there in the future.* I think Senator was pleasantly surprised that he did not have to drag me out kicking and screaming.

Staring out the window, I had my final glimpse of the White Mountains that so captivate me. The remainder of New Hampshire was gorgeous as well, but I knew my

---

* One night, while waiting in a carry-out restaurant, Senator and I were browsing one of the local real estate booklets. On the back cover, amid properties far above and beyond our budget, we were shocked to see our favorite bed and breakfast for sale. It was hard to imagine anyone doing as good of a job running it as the current owners. They were friendly, accommodating, easygoing, and extremely knowledgeable about the region. In addition to these qualities, they provided an excellent value for the price. Perhaps we could buy just our room?...

favorite spot. Heading south, we got to accidentally see Dartmouth College, thanks to Senator drinking too much coffee and water. It looked like it contained everything you would expect in a prestigious university-- well-preserved brick buildings with perfect trim and windows, lots of trees and ivy, small bustling lanes connecting campus buildings, and plenty of college-aged kids wandering around cluelessly while balancing coffee cups and smart phones.

Continuing our route westward, we crossed through Vermont and into New York. Incidentally, if you want to make good time, I-90 is the place to do it. The semis in the right lane are cruising at over 80mph, and it is assumed that cars will add another 10mph to that. When in Rome...

From Buffalo we curved south along Lake Erie, cruising through the northwest corner of Pennsylvania just before dusk. Because we apparently had not learned our lesson from the last time we traveled this way, we again found ourselves hotel hunting in eastern Ohio. Judging by the last experience, this meant we would exit the interstate multiple times, only to find that hotel signs led to either no rooms, ridiculously overpriced rooms, or absolutely filthy rooms. On this particular night, it was door #2. Though we have stayed in Lower Manhattan and Downtown Chicago, the most expensive room we ever paid for was outside of Cleveland, Ohio. Booo. It was clean and very comfortable, but certainly not fancy. The adage, "First time-- shame on you. Second time-- shame on me," was quite fitting. This time we made a collective vow, with each other as witnesses, to never get stuck in eastern Ohio without a reservation again.

*   *   *

When one does go to bed in eastern Ohio, assuming nothing especially bizarre has happened, one wakes up in eastern Ohio the next morning. We did, and upon doing so, found renewed motivation to get home. We were in the gateway to the flyover states, and there was no reason to linger. In less than forty-five minutes we were out the door and on the road. Senator took the wheel, and time was on our side as we crossed into Indiana and then Illinois. I missed New Hampshire already, but I was glad to get to my own home. I had things to do, anyway. As I sorted the mound of laundry, I also began to sort out ideas for our next big trip. Europe would certainly stretch my research capabilities...

Afterword

At last I did it. With the help of my Essential Other, I finally completed a personal goal of visiting each of the fifty states. From a beach in Florida to a glacier in Alaska, and from a forest in Maine to a volcano in Hawaii, we had logged more miles and footsteps than I could count. It did not represent any special talent on our part, but it felt like an accomplishment nonetheless. (Blame my grandparents and parents for the obsession.)

Just as exhilarating as visiting state #50 was returning to my favorite state. As a goofy, romantic girl growing up, I developed a new crush every time we visited a new region of the country. In most cases, they were dropped as soon as we went somewhere else. When I was six, we went to Wisconsin for the weekend. Though I remember being disappointed that it did not instantly look different upon crossing the border, (and that there was no actual border line painted across the highway, for that matter,) by seven I had decided to move there. In junior high we visited grandparents in Ontario, passing through Minnesota. I started to think maybe Wisconsin wasn't far enough north. Then came the big trip west when I was in high school. Breathtaking Colorado drew me under its spell... until I saw New England the next year.

This time I was sucked in irrevocably. Ocean, mountains, forests, waterfalls, hills, small towns, historical sites, a Euro-appreciative culture and more stole my heart. From the age of sixteen, the only thing that fluctuated was which specific New England state I targeted. As an adult, taking into account various economic, ideological, logistical, and political factors beyond simply look and feel, I narrowed down my dream destination to New Hampshire. Another trip to the White Mountains only solidified this.

I do hope to live in The Granite State someday, but in the meantime, I'm entrenched in The Prairie State. Time continues to fly by as we stay busy with jobs, a home, and many interests. Oh yes, and there is always travel...

~Wendy V
April 2015

Appendix A:
Dick Giracco Memoir

The following is a transcript of Dick Giracco's statements, as told to us when we met him at the Pacific Aviation Museum on Ford Island at Pearl Harbor. The first two recall his account of the Pearl Harbor attack, and the third is an explanation of his education background:

#1 I was stationed on Ford Island in Hangar 54, which was a headquarters patrol wing, too, that had Catalina flying boats like this one [*indicates his shirt*]. And unfortunately for us, that was the Japanese's first target, and the object being they wanted to get rid of all these long range sea planes so they couldn't go out and look for the Japanese fleet. So they attacked our sea planes and [*word unclear*] all at the same time, and that didn't take very long.

Then they concentrated on our fleet, and what got our attention first was the dive bombers making the noise coming down. We thought it was the Army Air Corps playing tricks on us. They used to come by every once in a while and dive-bomb us and drop flowers, and uh, make a big mess. So we went out to the front of the hangar to see... to take a look at it, and looked up and didn't realize they were Japanese, because they were the same colors as the Army Air Corps planes. Then when they dropped their bombs and pulled out from their dive, we seen the rising sun on the wings. Then we knew we were in big trouble.

[*phrase unclear, perhaps "An air of"*] self preservation,

and what I remember most about the whole attack was tremendous noise, and the concussion from things exploding. And as luck would have it, they were putting in a pipeline of some sort in between the [*word unclear*], and the runway. And it stretched all the way from the water down past the hangar where it is now. And it was about five or six feet deep, so everybody got in that ditch and had a ringside seat for the rest of the attack.

First attack lasted about an hour, and it stopped, and we thought it was all over. We got out for about fifteen or twenty minutes. Second wave come over and we ran in the ditch and stayed there 'till it was over with-- about two hours altogether. And that pretty much took care of that.

And after that, it was was just a matter of getting out and surveying all the damage and trying to get our sea plane ramp cleaned up so we could fly our airplanes again. And another side note that there was about eighty-seven or eighty-eight of these Catalina fighter boats on the island. Of that bunch, only four of them survived, and three of them were three planes that we had launched earlier that morning at five o'clock. They flew over to Maui and what they were doing over there was checking out the feasibility of refueling from the submarine. And we were just waiting for them to come back, mind you. Japanese got there, and that pretty much covers it.

#2   It was [word unclear] staging area for all these people coming off the battleships. And once we did get back in, then we had to put up with all that cleaning up and the battleship rolling around. It was a terrible mess. Of course, the Oklahoma being inverted, they were searching for people in there for about a week, and they made their way up to the bottom of the ship, tapping on that. And they'd have people listening all the time for people that were entrapped in the hull of the ship, and they rescued quite a few of them. And that was a mess. And I guess what I remember the most about the whole affair was the noise--tremendous, tremendous noise and concussion.

#3   They asked me why I quit [school]. They don't believe me when I tell them. I said, "Because I didn't have any clothes to wear." I had no clothes. I had one set, and whatever I had on my back was all I owned. I got tired of that, so I said I gotta' find something else [phrase unclear]. I quit school. I got my high school diploma later on when I was in the Navy, so that took care of that.

Appendix B:
Kailua Update

It appears we have jinxed another vacation spot. In November 2013, the Associated Press ran an article titled "Hawaii Town to State: Stop Sending Tourists Here". The gist of it was that many residents of Kailua, Oahu, (where we stayed,) are upset that tourists have started to discover it. They prefer to shun visitors who, like us, seek a quieter, natural alternative to the plastic tackiness of Waikiki. Apparently we have ruined their lives. An excerpt appears below:

> ..."Neighbors don't like having a stream of strangers staying next door. It doesn't feel like a neighborhood when you don't know the people there," board member Lisa Marten said. "If there's any sort of safety issue, there's no one to ask for help because you don't know them."...
>
> ...So when the board noticed the tourism agency's website suggested that "a Kailua vacation rental can be the perfect solution" for those planning a family vacation..., they decided to push back. By a 12-2 vote, the board in September passed a resolution requesting that the agency "stop promoting Kailua as a tourist destination and alternative to Waikiki"...

Well alrighty then. Aloha!

www.ingramcontent.com/pod-product-compliance
Lightning Source LLC
LaVergne TN
LVHW041618070426
835507LV00008B/326